MW00638852

VENS

Create Your Most Delicious Life

Life's a Bitch,
Especially Now,
Make it a JOY!

Create Your Most Delicious Life

Copyright © 2022 by Jill R. Stevens

All rights reserved under the Pan-American and International Copyright Conventions. This book may not be reproduced in whole or in part, except for brief quotations embodied in critical articles or reviews, in any form or by any means, electronic or mechanical, including photocopying, recording, or by any information storage and retrieval system now known or hereinafter invented, without written permission of the publisher, JOYful Goat Publishing.

ISBN (hardback): 978-1-957841-03-8
ISBN (paperback): 978-1-957841-09-0
ISBN (ebook): 978-1-957841-00-7
ISBN (audible): 978-1-957841-01-4

This book is dedicated to the real you—the one stepping into the light, *unapologetically*.

The hiders-in-plain sight. The closeted creatives.

The me who outgrew those ways of being.

Contents

0: Prelude - 1

1: Invitation - 23

2: Pulling Threads - 83

3: The Stories You Tell Yourself - 137

4: Changing the Story - 193

5: Telling a New-to-You Story - 247

6: Living Your Delicious Life - 297

7: Living Your Story Out Loud - 353

8: More Delicious JOY - 397

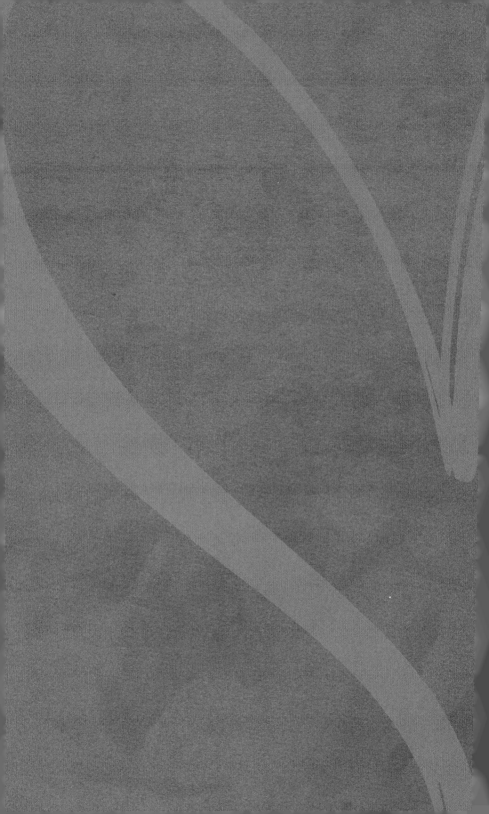

0: Prelude

Dear Fabulous Reader,

Before you dive deeply into these pages, I want to set the stage. Our stage.

Imagine for a moment a single sofa, capable of seating three, yet for just you and me.

Comfortably angled just so.

Center stage of whatever room makes you feel utterly relaxed. Perhaps your own living room, a dreamed-of library nook, or even out on a big wraparound porch.

This fantastic place will be your new reader-home. A space that, while expansive, feels deeply *intimate, homely, safe,* and mystically sunlit.

There's even a cashmere throw for those moments when you just need to snuggle in. Plus, a place for that mug of Joe, cup of tea, or brimming glass of whatever is your specialty.

As you flip a page, you will notice that some essays come in a rush of page-turning fun while others need space to digest and absorb. To reflect on.

How you sink into this work is the Journey of You.

A JOYful span of moments where sometimes I'll be present in the pages you turn, in the offering of a *Purple Pen Practice*—

an interactive treat also available as a downloadable handbook which you can dive into by accessing right now.*

And at other times, it may feel as though I am sitting right there, at the other end of your sofa—

two long-lost friends deep in contemplative conversation.

This is your chance to laugh,
to shed a tear or two,
as all these words
have been written
specifically for you . . .

with my very own purple pen.

My weapon,
my color,
my expression
of choice.

Done with love and JOY in the sincerest of desires that this work enables you to *find your voice* and begin *creating* and *living* what I myself do—

A Most Delicious Life.

jill

* http://www.thejoyfulwriter.com/book/delicious

JOY is the Journey of You

disclaimer

My default setting is JOY.

Creator, I am.
Creator, so are you.

birthright

Who are you when no one is telling you who to be?

I mean, NO ONE. Not even yourself.

Who are you subconsciously? *Unconsciously?*
Naturally?

Without all the layers . . .
all the copycat-is-me ways of being.

Without all the tall tale—
stories.

Without those low moments focused on
measuring up . . . ?

What is your default setting? Do you even know?

If you're like so many people,
you may be walking around without a clue.

Not because you're slow or forgot,
but because no one introduced the idea to you—
yet.

default

Your default setting is typically one of your highest values.

That thing that makes you *hum* and enJOY a secret smile of delight.

It's that place where all *aligns, flows, feels oh-so deliciously right.*

For many of us, it has been a *looong* time since we thought about our default setting, if it's even a concept that's entered our head.

This is something children tap into *instinctively.*

This is the place from which they show up—
happy, JOYful, curious, full of wonder.

All delicious defaults. No *intentional* thought to be this way or that.

Yet, adults, that's an entirely different—
beastly, tangled, mangled
ball of string.

Many people, especially women, spend so much energy, so much of their lives, living out someone else's stories of themselves.

We end up losing who we truly are in this effort to please, get along, be what everyone wants us to be, not even seeing how that's the thing eroding the very foundation of who we are.

Who we desire to be.

We tend to own, not the stories we choose for ourselves, but the ones that were handed down to us or imposed on us.

It's rude to talk back.
It's aggressive to have an opinion.

Be a good girl.
Sit up straight.
Don't talk too loud.

Boys don't cry.
Suck it up, Buttercup.

Now that last one I utter to this day, in jest, as a way to remember—

Be who you wanna be, Jill!

But the dilemma is, how many of us have *no fucking clue who that even would be?*

I know a few years back, I sure as hell didn't know.

I got so very good at trying not to rock the boat that I capsized little old me.

I'm literally banging the table with my fist while I write
this.

It's not aggressive to take a stand,
to have an opinion,
to have a voice.
To use it loud and proud.

To say what's on your mind,
to shout out what's in your heart.

It's not wrong to rock the damn boat!

Because it's only when you rock the boat,
your boat, your way,

that you find *You*, start to know *You*—
take ownership and responsibility
for your own thoughts, stories, actions
and begin to feel your own strength.

All that people-pleasing keeps us from knowing
ourselves, keeps us stuck and weak.

All the doing and spinning,
overthinking and analyzing every little thing
before taking a step—

That is what starts the *slow leak*,
zaps any confidence,
steals the JOY,
your JOY.

Do you even remember what brings you JOY?

The further away you are from *yourself*, the further away you are from JOY.

And JOY is everything, because everything is energy.

JOY is the Journey of You.

And is a child's most natural setting 95 percent of the time.

JOY is our birthright . . .

And yet, *can you remember the last time you truly felt JOY?*

I'm going to stress this word because I know and live by a secret . . .

Abundance Follows JOY.

When you make JOY a *priority* in your day-to-day life, *all shifts.*

Your relationship with yourself, with others, Your health, your wealth, your career, your stories . . .

When JOY becomes your default setting—naturally all changes, brightens.

And leads to a most delicious life.

come closer

Before you turn the page, come closer, as I have a delightful secret I want to share.

A secret I ask you to keep close to your heart as you read.

JOY, like love,
transcends all.

JOY, like love,
is yours and yours alone to feel, sink into, express, experience, enJOY.

JOY, like love,
needs nothing outside yourself to be.

JOY simply is.

If you want some of that . . .
this book may just become your new bible.

In these pages, you will find a few of what I call *Purple Pen Practices*.

These are the pathways to inductively sinking into what I'm called to share.

Instead of in one ear and out the other—

(as if you were listening to me read these words to you)

what if all these words, the ones that resonate, that you choose—

imagine if those words, thoughts, concepts stuck like the craziest of glue?

How would your life change if you literally absorbed the JOY from which I write all that is here?

Sinking into each *Purple Pen Practice* as it arises in the pages, that is how you cement what I'm about to share—*if it resonates with you.*

On the next page is your very first *Purple Pen Practice.*

I suggest giving it a go as inductive learning, not the regurgitation of the classroom that most of us came to know and not to love.

Inductive learning is like the stove that heats up at a moment's notice.

There is no waiting, watching, wondering when—*damn it!*—the word-change will boil up within and come.

Instead, there is a click, a connection, a flow
from my JOYful purple pen
connecting all the dots
and leading you on this magical,
delicious

Journey of You.

And when you're itching for a more interactive experience with all the *Purple Pen Practices* in one delightful place . . .

they are yours to access in *The Purple Pen Practice Handbook:* A delicious companion to *Create Your Most Delicious Life.*

And absolutely free as you invested in this book.

Simply scan the QR code or go to the link below (*) and access your copy now by entering your name and email address.

*   https://www.thejoyfulwriter.com/book/delicious

JOY

You can live your most delicious life, a life in balance with yourself.

To do so, to walk every step in JOY, I invite you to first ask this delicious question:

What brings you JOY?

Set a timer for seven marvelous minutes and sink in, pen in hand, and see what comes through you, to you.

All that is received will allow you so much clarity on this journey to creating the most delicious life.

Need more time? Give yourself that gift today. It will pay off in spades.

And lead to more delicious JOY!

I recommend asking yourself this question on the daily as you are reading the pages of this book.

face-planting JOY

Sometimes we won't know what brings us JOY
anymore . . .

Until we're chatting with a friend,
perhaps driving by a public park,
time suddenly stands still.

Simply seeing those children running, laughing,
playing takes you back, way back to that time when
swinging *oh-so high* made you feel belly-flops of JOY.

And smile so-so wide.

Go all the way back to childhood with a smile.

Back to that pillow fight.
That late-night food fight.

*Was it grapes in the bridal suite one cold January
night?*

I kid you not.

Ah, how delicious to ping a friend with a few fast-
flying grapes.

Feel it?
That outward smile.
That inner tickle.

Lean into it right now.

That's what JOY feels like *for you*, in your body.

Not quite there yet, no sweat.

Consider that time you tripped and fell . . .
Was it into the pool?

Or maybe if you're like me, you were walking
backward on the sidewalk lining a New England street.

Talking and smiling at your dad, only to spin around
and face-plant into a parking meter.

Oh, wow.

Painful, yes, but funny? JOYful?
Well, that all depends on you, does it not?

In this case, me . . .

Looking the fool got you playing it cool?

Not me, in that moment, as I saw my dad's laughter
bubbling up once he realized I wasn't concussed.

And that I only wanted to cuss.

So I laughed and felt the outpouring of JOY in that
shared moment of me looking foolish, klutzy, kinda
dumb, honestly . . .

And my dad's JOY.

For me, JOY and laughter go hand in hand, but perhaps for you, it's more like that time you fell oh-so hard for that very first boy or girl.

Tap into those butterflies,
that lit-from-within feeling,

the way you couldn't help
but have a bounce in your step,
a sway of your hips.

A moment when you so wanted to *Breakfast Club* fist pump the air.

Focus on the JOY you've felt before,
not the idea that you are lacking JOY now.

When you do, JOYful magic will easily begin to show up daily for you.

journey of you

I said it once, without thinking.

JOY is the Journey of You.

And how cool is that?
J.O.Y.

Throughout these pages, I will ask a question as rich and potent as dark, melting chocolate—

What do you want?

That's big, broad.
For some, it may feel too *open-ended.*

If that ask freaks you out, like it once did me, grab yourself a cup of tea or something that tickles your fancy.

Because it's okay. I got you, Boo.

Simply sink in.

The coming words are for you, *specifically.*

want

Answer this question—*What do I want* right now?

Or even more to the point—*What would bring me JOY* right now?

We don't have to eat the entire elephant in one ginormous *first* bite.

It's not about having all the answers to living your most delicious life already. We've only just begun.

In fact, imagine for just a beat that it's not about having anything at all, but instead *being your all*.

Defined, understood, believed—only by you.

That right there is the hardest of things for most humans to grasp. A concept that it's not about having more things or doing more stuff, but about who you show up being each and every single day.

A falling in love with *that* you.

Accepting that you.
Self-caring that you.
Listening to that you.
Understanding that you.

Eventually knowing and unconditionally loving that you.

If you're living a story,
of *getting it right, perfect, first—*
consider what that's costing you.

That pressure cooker *go-go-go* way of being.

Is there JOY in that competitive streak of doing it the best, the fastest, getting it—*damn it*—even if it kills you, wears you out, makes you so very unhappy?

If you feel frozen, trapped, completely at a blank as to what brings you JOY, I feel you.

And I'm here, through these pages,
to help guide you . . .
Guide you back to your own natural default setting.

To your version of JOY.

I am, after all, The JOYful Writer . . .

(and JOYful Coach)

1: Invitation

An Invitation

Have you ever had that nudge,
a tingle, calling, desire.

A beckoning deep within
to do something—

Different.

Something others might think is crazy,
not practical, *un*stable,
financially *in*secure.

Maybe an urge to
start your own business . . .

Write a book . . .

Find your voice,
calling . . .

Live life your way . . .

No longer asking for permission.

This is your space to find *your way, your voice* . . .

To publish a story, your story, and see it
right over there . . .

On a Barnes & Noble bookshelf,
a bestseller list somewhere,
popping up in a Google search bar,
available 24/7 on Amazon.

Or simply in the pages of your own divine diary.

Showing up in your day-to-day life . . .
as you.

When you're ready to start creating your most
delicious life,
with a magical purple pen,

or your color of choice.

Turn the page and sink in,
because this is your time to shine.

beginnings

Writing has always played a key role in allowing me to create my most delicious life.

Much like my environment has always mattered to me, the act of writing has always been like a *sidekick, best friend,* and *main love interest* all rolled up into one neat, purple-pennable package.

A character, if you will.

One I got to love and hate and play with.
To scream at, work on, bleed with.

Now you may be thinking,
I'm not a writer.

You could be wondering,
*Have I ever felt that passionately about . . .
anything?*

*I mean, you said, "Bleed with it."
And, frankly, I'm a little scared.*

*Should I even read these words, waste my time, sink
into this book?*

Valid Qs.

The question I'd ask of you is—

Are you currently living your most delicious life?

If the answer is *Hell yeah!*, put this baby down and carry on with your fine self. You probably don't need what I've got to say.

My words, after all, are not for every single soul out there.

Unless curiosity has got a busy bee in your proverbial bonnet, then read on, friend . . .

Curiosity rocks, even George the monkey knew that.

And if your answer is *Delicious life? What?* this book is specifically for you.

Because creating your most delicious life
is not about *what you do*
but all about *who you choose to be.*

And after all that's here between these pages,
I guarantee the path to your most delicious flipping life—

a life where *abundance literally becomes your bitch,*
will be laid bare for you.

And, oh boy, I am rubbing my hands together in glee. *Seriously!*

And leave it up to you

to now tap into your own excitement
as you sink into these words and rekindle your
innermost dream,

which can,
with a turn
of the very last
page,
become
your most delicious
reality.

storyteller

I've been a writer for more than thirty years, a best-selling author for half that.

Most of my words have been written as a *ghost*writer for others or under pseudonyms, because as you will soon learn, I was very good at hiding in plain sight.

I share this because I live and breathe *the power of storytelling*.

And when you see just how many stories you tell yourself on the daily, well, you can flip that script and begin telling new ones that uplift you, bring you JOY, and create a most delicious life.

stories are energy

Each one has a charge.

An ability to bring up all those locked-away feelings,
all the stuffed-down emotions.

And those feelings, emotions, they are *energy in motion*.

How we *feel* propels us forward
or looking back
into the rearview
of what was.

Words penned, spoken, even thought.
Yep, more energy.

Everything is energy.

To change your reality, you *start* by changing your
stories.

That begins with an awareness of just how you talk to
yourself.

The words you use,
the stories you spin—
and spin,
again and again and again.

I live and breathe stories.
And I once *stewed* in stories of the past.

Stories that I relived, retold, over and over.
Stories I allowed to keep me stuck.

Until I uncovered, discovered that stories can be my very kryptonite or my saving grace.

And in these pages, I will share, teach, explain, even JOYfully coach you through—*yep, you guessed it*—stories!

tall tales

What stories are you telling yourself?

What stories are you telling about yourself?

Too many people, particularly women, get stuck in their stories.

Stories about our bodies.
How we ought to be in the world.

Who we should be, what we should do, how we should act.

Our stories can become a cage of playing by another's rules . . .

Our stories can keep us stuck, forever seeking . . .

Our stories can set us free.

It's a *choice*
to create a most delicious life,
one that only you hold the key to.

But so often our stories are a mixture of this and that.

A splash of what is expected,
what is heard,
what we are told.

33

A dash of what we think is desired
of us.

Until we wake up one day
neck-deep in a life
that feels like a never-ending spin
around a suds-filled,
front-loading washing machine—
cycle set to infinity.

I understand playing by another's stories,
following a set of rules,
simply trying to fit in and please all
or saying *screw it* and pleasing none.

I chose the People-Pleasing Path—

externally, less bumpy than Screw You Street,
but internally, just as detrimental.

As each step took me farther and farther
away from knowing me.

Pleasing me.

Being me.

selfish

This book is truly all about being selfish
because that is the only way to create your most
delicious life.

And being *selfish* is cloaked in such negative stories.

The word *so not* understood.

I was in my twenties when I shared with another,
someone "close to me," that I was going to focus on me.

To be a bit selfish for a beat.
To tap into what I wanted in my life, out of this life.
To tune out all the other voices, thoughts, opinions
and hear my own.

Even to press pause
in my natural tendency to
people-please, accommodate, help out.

My deep-rooted desire to focus on everyone else to
the point I'd forget about me.

Would have to deal with my own needs, issues,
desires, problems.

My deeply personal announcement was actually met
with horror, a dash of judgement, and name-calling.

I could say it shocked the hell out of me, but truly, part
of me knew better than to share what was so private—
especially while in it, unraveling it, discovering me.

See, this person truly believed I must be
a horrible person

to put myself first,
to take a moment and be selfish,
to focus on me,
to get to know myself.

When you sink into the truth that
selfish is not bad,

not right nor wrong
but is the path to loving you,
the ticket that makes *all* possible,
you too will see the bucket of stories you've been sold
your entire life.

Stories that you perhaps believed
to your own detriment. . .
just like me.

Newsflash:

There's enough sunshine for everybody.

You don't have to hide.
You don't have to *tone it down*.

Not during this read of these here pages,
and not ever again.

To be *you*,
the real *you* . . .

Buried under all the stories,
told,
shared,
believed,
retold . . .

Be *selfish* during your reading of this book.
Block time.

Make the *feeding* of you,
of your very soul,
the most important moments
of your day.

Every day.
If you don't, *who will?*

These pages, parts, paragraphs are all about that,
adding to your Soul "Bank" Account—

that place and space where your personal power
resides,
ignites,
grows,
smolders,
is not allowed to die.

Being selfish by caring for you and growing that Soul
Account to massive amounts

leads to *confidence*,

strokes those buried *dreams*,
makes creating each day a JOYful thing.

And enables you to create your most delicious life.

Which is why you're here, is it not?

So I leave you now to ponder this.

Who are you?

Hmmm, such a fabulous, breath-stealing question. One
we so rarely spend time diving into. Yet, this very ask
sets the stage for all you show up being.

Ask yourself today—*Who am I?*

Do you even know?

It takes a beat of selfish to get in the know.

identity

Everything you believe about *yourself*, *your past*, and *your future* is a story.

Everything.

That's deep. Let's dive in . . . *together*.

I once thought I was an awful, unlovable person.

It was something I heard several times from another.

One who knew me,
who was supposed to love me,
so I absorbed those words.

Was it true? Factual? *Hell no.* I was simply a child.

But I allowed myself to believe those words, to operate from them and create stories supporting them in my own head.

Stories that led to me believing
I can't be loved,
I'm not good enough.

The story where if I am so awful, how can I ever win at this game called life?

So instead of life supporting me, I saw life as *out to get me.*

These stories allowed me to sabotage myself at every turn. When life was going *too good*—that awful, unlovable-is-me story would rear its ugly, demented head, and my shit would *have* to hit the fan.

Meaning, I perfected the art of ruining a good thing because my story was one of undeserving.

You're here, and that means some part of you is ready to swim into the depths of you, to shed all those stories . . .

those layers of false pretenses and discover just who you really are under it all.

Because if you're like 99 percent of the population, answering that three-word question—*Who am I?*—would make your palms clammy, your mouth bone-dry and your mind scream something like . . .

I don't even know!

Welcome to the club . . .
of getting to know you.

A shared skinny-dip into a divine pond—
crystal clear, 78 degrees
(roughly 25 degrees Celsius for our international friends)
fed from the most *pristine, wondrous* spring.

A watering hole that will renourish and refresh your mind, body, and soul.

And I couldn't be more pleased.

Because this is the key to all.
To discovering you.

When you do, only then can you begin to create a life that simply lights you up.

A life that excites you,
hugs you daily,
supports you,
honors you,
fills you with JOY.

That is where we begin,
a three-letter word
that is my
e.v.e.r.y.t.h.i.n.g.

as you may have already come to see.

JOY

And for you is the fast-pass-forward into the depths of these pages . . .

JOY *stands for the* Journey of You.

boxed in

So often we box ourselves into
what we are *supposed* to be,
what we *should* be,
what we're *taught* to be.

We erect this box, a cage for one, with stories.

A cage so wide yet so narrow,
it spans forever out of sight
yet leaves no room in which to turn to or fro.

It confines even as we are *lost* in its massiveness.

A box most of us want desperately to break out of.

Yet, we sink into thoughts of *But how?*

Stories of fear.
But what's on the other side?

So many would remain trapped even if a knotted rope
were tossed over one never-ending side.

I say, it's time to shatter the fucking box.
Once and for all.

That is the only way forward.

To break the box you *must* first, selfishly, rediscover yourself.

By going on the *Journey of You*.
By once again learning to live in JOY.

By acknowledging
the *fear*,
the *stories*

and giving both
a double-fisted
F-you.

And by answering the question that simply terrifies most of us:

What do I really want?

When you're good and ready to climb on board, I have but one request . . .

Leave your Negative Nelly side behind. Give her paid leave, a holiday. And strip away all the layers she's donned throughout time.

You may not release them all at once. If you're like me and so many I've worked with, *readers*, you've built up quite a protective shell.

Heck, mine was reinforced steel, *I get you!*

But beating yourself up over not shedding fast enough what you've held onto for a lifetime—

Well, friend, those are simply grounds for a new, disempowering story to sprout.

Consider putting down the self-punishment stick . . .

Instead imagine, just for a hot sec, that this pool of untouched water,

the one we are about to play in together . . .

This natural spring of *You* will feel so incredible
caressing your *real* skin,
not all the layers you've worn
throughout your entire existence

But the *bare-is-you* version.

The true, skin-deep *You*.

So when you're *ready* . . . get *set* . . . it's time to *play*!

Strip away your first layer by saying *hell yes* to diving in with me!

It can be a big toe touch,
a skinny-dipping treat,
a deep, downward dive of delight,
or a hip-deep careful wade . . .

The *choice* is yours.

Ring the bell, toot your horn, and jump on board with me as this JOY Jill Train is pulling out of the station,

leaving your current reality and starting on the track
into a new dimension of you.

A place where you let go of all you once knew.

And when you do—*fully, completely*—
let go of those stories you currently see as your
absolute truth,

the same stories you may just love to hate,
keeping them around
like a favorite pair of threadbare, worn-to-soft jeans,

when you finally strip them off

you create your most delicious life.

And that is why you're here.

To break free of the boxed-in stories that no longer
serve you.

This is what you say,
in the dead of the night,
you want . . .

is it not?

frog killer

As a child, I loved frogs. All animals.

Creatures big and small were my playmates, my confidants, my best friends.

Still are if I'm being vulnerable, real.

I have always found it easier to share my secrets with a four-legged friend than the two-legged one who might

judge me,
stab me in the back,
or—God forbid—praise me.

Hmm, so many stories right there in that one line, don't you see?

But let's return to little old me at age six when I decided it was high time I swam with my frog-friends.

Off I went to the swamp close by and collected a few dozen small frogs from the murky, cool waters.

Slime didn't bother me, and frankly, I thought the little dudes were cute. So sloshing water from my nearly full bucket, making sure no frog was left behind, I trudged back with my load . . .

for bath time.

As the frogs gathered in my Snoopy pail, I ran the water as I'd seen the Bio Mom do endless times.

Being nice, because as an only child, I'd not yet learned this concept but heard it—*sharing is caring*—I dumped my frog-friends in.

Dirty water and all.

When the Bio Mom called, I ran out, shutting the door, light off, knowing they'd swim and play without me as I'd seen froggies do countless times before in the swamp.

Only a few minutes passed and I returned, ready to strip bare and climb in to dog paddle side by side with my twenty-four playmates.

Only to stare down into the bath water and find them belly up, floating. One by one.

It took me a minute,
a finger push to just one,
to clearly see they were all
dead.

Pulling back my hot finger, I knew immediately what I had done. I had burned my babies, forgetting to turn on both the hot and cold taps.

Tears sliding down my cheeks, I sat on the floor mat, staring into that tub of lightly green-gray water and cried as I waited for it to cool. Then one at a time, I collected bodies and rested them on top of the towel I'd folded at the bottom of my now Snoopy burial bucket.

Time and time again, I lowered one little, white-bellied frog in my small hands and placed him side by side with his friends, his family—sniffing and choking back sobs.

In that moment, I knew the truth. I was all the things I'd been told. *Bad. Horrible. Unlovable.*

In that moment, I became The Frog Killer.

And that story made me buy into the truth of another's story about me.

Suddenly, in my own mind, I was a bad, horrible, unlovable little girl.

I grew up and into womanhood never leaving that story behind—until one day, it no longer served me.

One day, in my late twenties, I let that story, that belief go and stopped being bad, horrible.

Unlovable.

That one took some time to untangle, as some entrenched tall tales do.

When I saw I was simply a child of six, not a *frog killer*, I saw that I wasn't *bad* nor *horrible*.

When I saw that what I had done was from a place of love, of simply wanting to play with my frog-friends that what happened didn't have to back up the harshly spoken words of an angry, upset adult . . .

Only then was I able to let that story of *bad, horrible me* go.

However, the belief or story that I was unlovable, that lingered on for a decade or more.

Deeply rooted in my core.

Supported by other tales, many moments that proved I was indeed not lovable as I'd once been told.

starting line

How do I start, Jill?

This is the question I have so often heard from my decades working with creatives and is as simple to answer as this.

The *how* is none of your business.

You simply start.
Pen or pencil to a piece of paper—*writing*. That's how.

Whoa, girl! But I'm not a writer, Jill.

I say you don't need to be,
but if you desire the fastest path forward—
it's the *Write Way*.

Pen to paper,
you start.

Notice the old story.

Hit a mental stop
or end your verbatim retelling mid-share.

Mentally or physically, begin to craft a new story to tell.

One that *serves* you.

Remember, everything is energy.
Everything is also a story.

Your stories can either lift you up on high
or drag you *way down low*.

If you're an auditory processor—
don't much like pen and paper,
always on the go . . .

Access a voice-recorder app on your phone and start
talking to yourself.

This is *your* Write Way path.

Talking to yourself can be incredibly therapeutic.

You'll find the answers to many of your own questions
simply by *speaking out loud*, even—*especially*—with no
one listening.

At least I do. And it was in the verbalizing, vocalizing,
that I heard my own patterns of self-abuse.

In speaking out loud my thoughts, hearing the words
flow in my own voice, things I'd not say to my worst
enemy, I was able to see just how much self-hate I
actually carried around within me.

Through my own voice, I quickly tapped into my
stories of *not good enough, the world is out to get me,
something must be wrong with me,* and so many more.

Hearing myself speak allowed me to let these stories go.

And it all starts by hearing and seeing that—*yes!*—
everything is a story, then shedding stories that no
longer serve you to make room for new stories that *do.*

And it starts by you
repeating a new story,
your new story,
over and over and over again.

Seeing it as your reality.
Seeing it as your possibility.

Seeing you as that which you say you are already.

Even—and this is *key*—when you have no concrete,
solid-as-a-rock proof, *yet.*

Storytelling, in whatever form it takes, is actually *an art*
you have been *perfecting* your entire life.

Perhaps not (yet) as a writer.

But stories you do tell. We all do.

They are inescapable.

Stories about
your abilities,
your looks,
your ways of being,
your flaws,
your wins,
your limitations—

just to name a few, my friend.

Our stories create our beliefs . . .

All you believe
first started as a little,
itty-bitty baby-story
told to you,
spun by you,
mastered by you.

You're already a master storyteller, can't you see?!

blank page

For those who *think* you cannot write,
I say stop flattening your soufflé!

Everything is a story.

Even—*I can't write*—is a story.

I'm a bad writer is a choice to
say, repeat, believe
which then can become . . .
Yep, a story.

If you choose to put your attention and your belief in
the story of being a bad writer, guess what? You're a
bad writer because *you say you are.*

Remember, I was
not smart enough
not pretty enough
not thin enough
not worthy of love

 . . . until, suddenly, I was.

I simply chose to accept and begin to tell myself a *new*
story.

And at first, it was *weird, unfamiliar,* and *uncomfortable.*
It felt like a lie, until *suddenly* it did not.

It took falling in love with the discomfort.

The key is to keep telling yourself the *new* story—*over and over again.*

It all starts with you.
And ends with you too.

If you don't want to be a bad writer,
or a bad parent,
a sad person,
a failure . . .

It may sound too simple,
creating a new story to tell. . .

as most *for-sure* things are,
but it's the *first step* to a new path.
A new *you*.

And that's fabulous news.

For it means when you are ready,
the story of you,
the *Journey of You*,
can begin again—anew.

Because you can change your story.

excavation

Writing is such a very powerful tool.

A tool, a skill that anyone able to pick up a pen, type on a keyboard, use thumbs on a smartphone screen can do.

For some, *writing words* or *thoughts* is easy.
For others, it may feel hard, uncomfortable.

Yet, I tell you what, it's *the cheapest form of therapy* out there.

And has the power to change how you see your very world.

And yes, I am biased as I am a writer.

I've also taught writing to thousands of children and adults, and the skill never fails to benefit.

Whether it be a daily one-page essay at the start of class, or helping a new or established author workshop their words, writing is a skill, an art form, that can change your life.

Not writing that best-selling novel.

Nope, although maybe, one day, for you.

What I'm talking about here is writing new stories that support the new you.

And the most delicious life you are here to create.

Look, if you're here, chances are you are seeking something—perhaps the title of this book, to create a more delicious life.

Perhaps to attract more JOY
and abundance
into your life.

To let go of those shit stories that imprison your very soul.

To craft some anew that fulfill you.

It's possible.

All it takes is an *excavation* of what was, what's buried in the way.

A *willingness* to go there.

Only when you let go of those things,
stories that no longer serve you,
can you truly make room to create new ones that do.

I started to write the stories in my conscious mind, and in my journal, as they popped up.

I became a mad scientist—paying attention to what was playing on repeat in my own head.

In writing out these stories, I saw where my attention was, and it was no wonder things in my life, at times, looked grim.

Perhaps you, too, can relate?

A few of my stories that I journaled out included:

- *I'm not enough.*
- *I need to be fixed.*
- *I'm broken.*
- *Tone it down, Jill.*
- *Don't share; it leads to pain.*
- *I need XYZ to be happy.*
- *No one will love me.*
- *Why does he love me?*
- *What does he really want?*
- *I'm a big, fat failure.*
- *Fraud.*
- *Liar, liar, pants on fire.*
- *Copycatter.*
- *Useless.*
- *Worthless.*
- *Life's out to get me.*
- *God's punishing me.*

And the list goes on and on and on.

But hear me loud and clear. All this was playing—
automatically—in the background of me, running
even as I breathed in and out. Often *unbeknownst* to
conscious me, the supposedly *aware* me.

All my *decisions* and *choices* and *ways of self-
sabotage* were first *filtered* through these programs—
these stories.

Stories constantly running behind the scenes of me.

But, instead, I lived and breathed . . .

these absorbed stories, accepted beliefs,
as my truth.

But with awakening
to what I was internally saying
to myself on repeat,
came *choice*.

The ability to now *flip the script*. To *choose* in this
moment to *accept* or *reject* the story of

*I too have fat thighs. I must, as mine are pale just like
hers.*

I can now *choose* to say, *it's okay for believing that lie.*

For thinking, *Well if she talks like that about herself,
and she's the adult, then that's how it's done.*

This was my story to flip.

What's your old, tired story—perhaps also one from childhood—that could use a good flip?

Not feeling like you're *good enough, lovable even* because of the way people treat you.

How they reject you,
leave you,
turn on you,
betray you,
maybe even beat you down . . .
with words,
with energy . . .

What if you have trained people to show up for you in that way?

What if you not *loving yourself*—knowing you are enough, are the very things leading them down that path to see you in that vein?

Might sound harsh, but it's so very true.

When I got this, I began down the empowering path of boundaries, of retraining, of no longer tolerating that which did not enrich me, better me, support me.

I can now let old stories go without *blame*, without *shame*, as those feelings simply lead to more stories that put me on the *Suffering Train*.

Excavating stories takes time for some.

Or one can create an avalanche,
clearing the forest of stories that no longer serve you
at forest-fire speed.

Just one tall tale once believed
and now cut off at the knees
can bring down so many more.

one fell swoop

One way of letting go is not better than the other; it's simply the way that's best for you, in this moment, as you too allow the stories to drop and fade away . . .

Imagine what could grow in place of those old tales if you simply allowed each to gently go into the dawn of the newly awakened you—*one by one* or *in one fell swoop.*

Now that's a delicious thought.

And if you're anything like I used to be, you're wondering

how to make it happen,
how to speed it up,
how to just do it now, already!

Oh, patience was so *not* my strong suit; I feel you.

Just know you are exactly where you need to be on this *Journey of You.*

A journey truly not about the *how*, not about the *speed* but sinking into the *process* and *allowing* one story at a time.

The desire to rush it and get it done, get somewhere new . . .

Imagine if that too is a story.

Imagine the only place to be is right where you are. In it.

Whatever it is for you.

What I have found for me was that knocking
down one story that no longer served me often
automatically created a free fall for other stories to
topple and go.

And that right there freed me to enJOY where I was.

To stop my perpetual need to chase,
to be anywhere but the present moment—

with myself.

One such story, which led to many others tumbling
down like laid-out dominos on a tropical Little Haiti
morning, is perhaps a common one for so many . . .

What if I'm not good enough?

If this is a story you resonate with,
are repeating about yourself
on some big or small level—
this next vignette is for you.

.

enough

I spent the majority of my early and adult life *hiding* the bone-deep belief that I *knew* I wasn't good enough.

That I was lacking, that I wasn't lovable—as me. Because who was I, really?

Then I found this amazing, annoying, funny, cynical, handsome, logical Frenchman.

And he loved me.

Instead of sinking in,
instead of enJOYing him, his love,
I questioned it at every turn.

Why does he even love me?

I could sit here and ponder what made me go down this path, to have had so little self-confidence and self-esteem as to question the love of the man I'm with.

And I have.

That is one deep, dark, twisted path that led me in all-consuming circles.

Instead, what if the path ends with the awareness that this story, belief, tall tale I spun in my little old head does not serve me.

Perhaps, at one point it did.

Yet, at some point, I had to ask myself—

Is it worth my time, diving into that bottomless pit and pulling at the plug of why *simply to swirl and swirl and swirl?*

Or focus instead on the *possibility* that *I am enough.*

why

I used to wonder why my mother didn't seem to like me, *love me.*

I would ponder what I did wrong,
why I wasn't good enough for her,
and what I could change in me
that would make her finally
see me,
hug me,
love me.

Want to like me,
pretty please . . .

All my energy centered early in life around *why*.

Exhausting me.

In the classroom, *why* was a good thing.

When you ask

Why are the stars hanging in only the night sky?
Do they really sleep during the day?
I want to sleep with the stars, not under them!

You are smiled at and perhaps patted on the head or
indulged by an adult's time, attention.

Ah, rewarded.

Why as a child is cute.
Why as a student is praised.

Why as a teen can become obnoxious and easily overlooked by a busy parent as every sentence can start with that three-letter word.

Why can't I go out with Johnny?
Why can't I date, Mom?
Why can't I get my license?
Why can't I stay up?
Why do they hate me?
Why am I so fat and ugly?

Why as a teen can begin one down a disastrous path.

A preoccupation with forever asking,
analyzing,
questioning
the very thing
that doesn't even matter.

Why?

Forever spinning, depleting, doubting.

Left to create stories around that *why*.

Asking *why* is the equivalent of a wormhole. A trip down an uncharted place in space no one, up till now, has ever been.

Forever stuck in *why* is the same journey to nowhere but worry, unease, unrest, and likely dis-ease.

Does asking *why* a woman didn't love me, as a child, as a teen, as an adult help me or allow me to sink deep into possible scenarios . . . ?

Possible tales that support, answer my very own ask.

> *I must not be enough.*

> *I must not be lovable.*

> *I must not be who she wants me to be.*

What if I change me? Will that then do the trick?

> *Oh, but why am I not enough?*

> *Why am I not lovable as me?*

> *Why must I change?*

A three-letter word that creates a massive, twisted loop.

At least it did for me. What about for you?

Because I felt oh-so lacking,
forever responsible for the actions and reactions of
another . . . of a mother.

Believing that if I was only better, somehow someway,

that things would be as I desired—that I'd be enough, that I'd be loved as me—

was my road to constant misery.

So I learned to hide the important pieces of me—*in plain sight.*

I learned to lock down that which I did not want tainted by my natural instinct to believe I wasn't good enough.

I perfected the art of compartmentalizing that which brought me JOY so that I could not be snuffed out in the broad daylight or a dark, lonely night.

Hiding in plain sight became my saving grace, my unshared secret.

The endless squeeze of the very best hug from your very best friend.

It was warm, delicious, and *mine all mine.*

But like all good things, there are two sides to each story-coin.

And hiding my light,
while allowing myself to only *secretly* shine bright
also kept me playing ridiculously small.

closeted creatives

If you're ready to create new stories *and* your most delicious life, then be all in with me and you may be shocked by just who you become at the end of our time together.

Or this may just be our beginning.

I have worked with many people professionally and personally, yet the ones I tend to attract are typically hiders-in-plain sight, like the former me, or *closeted creatives*.

Those who chose a path of security,
of doing what they *should* do,
were *supposed* to do,
and suddenly wake up one day
feeling an overwhelming sense of lack.

As though a fundamental piece of themselves is missing.

Perhaps you can relate.

Most who come my way simply feel *called* to work with me, and I often hear them say

I'm not sure I even want to write a book.
But I want your energy.

I want your JOY!
I want what you're having!

And then a funny thing happens.

Over a few months, as we work together, tapping into what feels off, stuck, out of order for them, my clients literally *find their voice.*

Their JOY . . .

And nine out of ten times it's the voice of a creative soul buried under stories of *should do this or that* instead of simply tuning into the artist within.

One's true voice is impossible to tone down forever.

It's the voice that's laid dormant but has always been.
Calling to you in your dreams.
Peeking out between those *have-to* moments.

A voice that can only be restrained when we *tap out* of being our truest self, stuffing down emotions in order to play the game of life by another's rules.

Amazing things happen when we allow ourselves to feel all those pent-up, bottled-up, stored emotions.

To *name* them, *honor* them, *allow* them to be present.

Suddenly we rekindle the *motion* of that dream within.

More than half of my coaching clients end up doing a one-eighty within a few months and commonly say something like, "Jill, I think I want to write a book after all!"

That is the *power* of feeling what's not been felt recently, if ever.

While this book may be picked up by some writers, artists, and closeted creatives, it's truly for the you who wants to live *your* life *your* way—*finally*.

If you want that, you're in just the *right* place.
At just the *right* time.

Even if you never want to write a book . . .

To write nothing more than
the private words in your journal . . .

Or simply take part in the offered Purple Pen Practices within . . .

That's perfect too.

The point is to *discover* your stories.
To feel those feelings.

To release all that bottled-up energy
and set yourself in motion once again.

Armed to the teeth with new tales.

And often, we do this best when we write it out.

magic infinity

There is no magical destination,
only a series of magical moments.

There is no *there*.
There is simply *where you are.*

Yes, have a goal.
But don't become so caught up in obtaining it
that you forget the right here,
the right now.

A goal is simply a *target* on the *forward path* of you.
A place to focus, to reconnect to.

A goal without a plan and
some course correction every now and then
is nothing more than a fantasy.

Personally, I love the idea of an *Infinity Day* goal.

Not a new concept but one I heard years ago and was
just reintroduced to recently by an amazing, extremely
accomplished woman who lives her best life each and
every day.

This is a goal, a look-see, of your *ideal* day . . .

The day when life just clicks,
all makes sense,
and you are living The Dream.

Your Dream.
A most delicious life.

When you stop thinking
in six months,
next year,
when I meet this certain criteria in my head
then I'll have made it . . .

Only then will you actually begin to enJOY your life.

Fuck no!

EnJOY *this* moment now.
Feel JOY now, reading these words.

Smile and know that you got this thing called life by the short and curlies and you're taking it for a JOYride.

You are *choosing* to create your most delicious life each and every moment.

Life is nothing more than a series of moments.

Moments most people *miss* because they're *seeking something more.*

Something better, bigger, badass-ier than what currently is.

There is only *now*.
Right now.

Miss it?

Ask yourself,

Who do I want to be right now?

And start there.

Deal with the stories that come up for you *in this moment,*

not *all the stories* of every moment of your life.

Learn how to feel the emotions welling in you, if there are any, in this moment.

In each moment.
No judgement.

Simply allow,
with grace.

Sad? *Cry.*

Mad? *Go punch a pillow.*

Feeling down? *Dance it out.*

You have so much more power than you know,
when you place your attention on the now.

Not in the rearview mirror of you

And not so far down the road
that you miss the opportunities
just up ahead.

Purple Pen
PRACTICE

infinity day goal

Purple pen out your Infinity Day goal and see what a perfect day in the life of you would look like, feel like, smell like, sound like, taste like, be like.

An Infinity Day goal is not about looking forward without paying attention to where you are.

Instead, consider it a blueprint on a large one-dimensional sheet of crisp, freshly inked paper . . .

filled with all the infinite possibilities of your coming attractions.

It's the plan that, detailed out, shows you where to build the foundation that will best serve this newly becoming you.

And creating this blueprint-to-you fills your being with so much wonder.

Just playing in all the minute and grand-scale ideas without getting tripped up on any one thing.

Imagine for a moment, you slip awake each morning—
and the first thing you do
before you even open your eyes,
give a little stretch,
curl your toes, and flip back the covers . . .

77

Even before that morning set of push-ups,
the delicious fresh brew, or
blending of that green shake . . .

Before those sneakers grace your feet
and you pound the pavement, trail, or treadmill
at a stroll, a delicious heart-pumping pace, or a
graceful gallop . . .

Imagine that the very first thought that enters your
consciousness is *utter, absolute, divine gratitude* for
this day.

There it is .. . the smile.

Another beautifully aligned day where you get to
wake up with a shit-eating grin, knowing you got this,
whatever comes your way.

Because you got you.

You love you. And you feel that love within before you
even crack a grin . . . a warmth, a blooming bone-deep.

Feel that smile radiate right now . . . sprouting first
inside, so deep you hold your hand to your heart so
the JOY deep down doesn't burst out in a magnificent
kaleidoscope of light.

You hold it in and allow it to shine upon each and
every one of your cells,

healing you,
clearing you,

building you
up, up, up.

A rebirth, an *awakening figuratively and literally* each and every day.

This˙ is your Infinity Day, how it all begins.

Your knowing that you are but a drop of water in the ocean of all that is.

A drop
no longer disconnected
from understanding, dare I say knowing,
it is part of the whole.

You are one with all and so *you rise, you shine, you make impact* on this day from a place of loving you unconditionally.

You set your feet on the floor with *intention*—rooted, grounded, *oh-so very blessed.*

This is your Infinity Day, where even when things seem off, go sour, that doesn't affect you.

You never sway from your true, inner knowing of you.

You choose peace over drama.
You choose love over self-hate.

You choose your words and thoughts with care because you *know* on this day you have so much power in the palm of your small or large hand.

You have so much power in the words you speak, think, feel within . . .

And you protect you, *boo*, by choosing those words that *uplift, empower, support* you and all those you come in contact with.

Now you do you.

Paint the picture of your Ideal Day—this is your Infinity Day goal.

What your most delicious of days will look like, feel like, be like.

And as you draft it, craft it . . .
know that it already is.

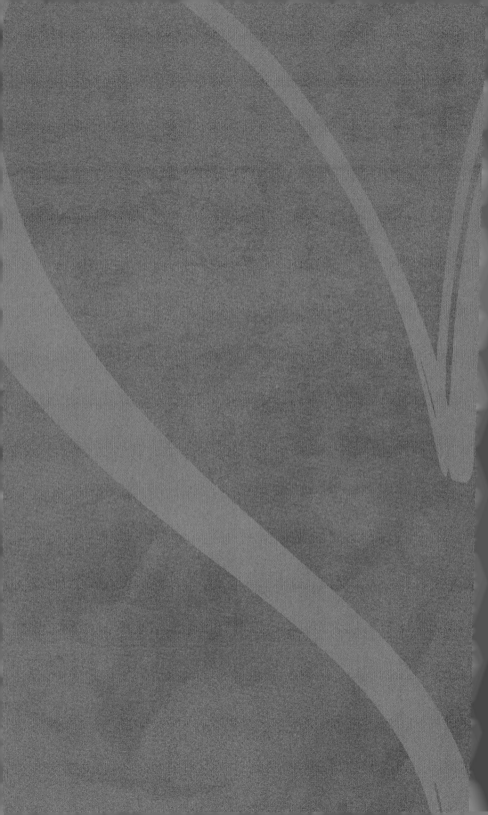

2: Pulling Threads

Pulling Threads

Everything is a story.

To find the story, all you have to do is *pull the thread.*

For example, what do you *believe in*?

What do you truly believe?

About yourself,
the world,
everything,
anything.

Imagine if what you believe
isn't known, confirmed, #truth
but simply an automatic, automated response,

a program running in the background of you?

belief

We spin our beliefs from the stories we buy into,
believe, own as our own.

And some beliefs are handed down like an older
sister's ill-fitting clothes.

I never had one of those, an older sister, so personally,
I have no sibling stories.

No middle child *woe is me.*
No *spoiled baby* of the bunch.

However, I do relate to stories of being *an only.*

A solo child who discovered early on
how to spin tales
like the glistening web
of a most creative,
early morning
spider.

Tales to entertain—*me.*

As I spent most of my time alone
with four-legged forest friends
and my insatiable imagination.

I pondered stories around

Where do I belong?
Do I even fit in?
Will anyone like me?

I heard stories of

Be more ladylike.
You're too sensitive.
Tone it down, Jill.
Children are seen, not heard.

Perhaps you can relate.

born again

I remembered sitting there,
on a hard pew,
week after week,
wondering about this
oh-so angry God.

This burn-in-hell,
fire-and-brimstone white dude with a beard,
forever dressed in a robe,
as he seemed to always be portrayed at the time.

A god who wanted to *punish, hurt,*
to press down into the soil of redemption
the me who was too *sinfully* human.

And yet, here I was *created in his image.*

Confusing to say the least.

Yet, the *expectation* was to confess my sins each
Sunday and be forgiven.

Understanding *not* required.

I remember listening, digesting, and *rejecting those
stories*, knowing within me a different tale of, "That's
not *my* god."

See, *I chose* to believe there was *a god, a being, a force* even as early as five, six, seven years old.

I chose to have faith in something outside of me.

Even as I was oh-so slowly taught
and forgot
to have faith

in me.

Taught this by the very ones surrounding me each and every Sunday.

Give it to God became the go-to instead of personal responsibility.

God's Will, God's Way became the slogan for *no need to change.*

But nonetheless,
this creator of The All—
he, she, it,
why must we categorize, label, classify?

For me, that being was *Benevolent, JOYful, Loving* and so not about punishment.

My god was all about betterment.

Was about *when you pray, you move your feet.*

I chose a new story from the one I was being told.

Something in me knew to reject the story
I was being sold
and I listened to that sweet voice within . . .

calling out,
shouting out,
warning me

of a story that did not feel true
to me.

Hello, inner knowing. Nice to meet you.

**Notice where you too may have done
this . . . had a similar *feeling.***

As it's powerful to recognize when we *reject* stories
that simply *do not align* with who we are at our core.

That's recognizing the real you.

Even when we feel we don't truly know ourselves,
we often know enough to say,

Ah, hell no.

And that is something to *lean* into.

That is *your* everything.

It was seated in those hard pews week after week,
singing songs with little tone and somehow little hope,
I felt the lack of JOY. I saw the flaw of mankind.

I watched heads nod. I heard *Amens!* tossed about,
the Bible thumping, even a few sobs now and then.

One minute tears glistened the eye, a message hitting
home, only to be repeated again and again and again.

I saw with this angry God present in one's corner there
was no need for personal responsibility—not when all
would be forgiven again.

I learned that with this *punishing god,* present in
another's sphere, left was no room for discussion as all
was "His way."

As a child, a mini-me observer, I saw firsthand irony
and hypocrisy. Not by all . . .

But by enough to cry foul—
and not want to play ball.

That inner knowing is as unique to you as your own
thumbprint or strand of DNA.

It can show up as
a sound,
a voice,
a recurring dream,
a feeling deep within.

It can be a loss of voice when you refuse to speak.

This is how my inner voice gives me a good
smackdown when I don't say my *peace.*

Our stories, our feelings, they are stored in our very cells.

Even science is now climbing aboard the *inner* workings of just how amazing we human beings are.

Imagine for a moment what that means.

Your stories live on within you at a cellular level . . .

You've probably experienced this but not given it more than a passing thought.

How your body remembers stories, places, times— especially on an emotional level.

Just how easily you can be transported back to that moment and space.

Are you feeling me?

frigging dishes

In my early years, I grew up in an environment where arguing was communicating. Now I see just how *ineffective*, *inefficient*, and *back-assward* that is.

But back then I was simply modeling what I knew with my own Frenchman.

We were on an island, much like how we met but no longer full of that honeymoon-like, island-hopping awesomeness.

Instead, we were *in* life, a life we had created together and one I resisted at each and every turn.

Let me take you to that moment in time

My hands in water, banging dishes as I *washed* them with force.

Frigging *dishes*.

Steaming internally.
Flushed externally.
Mumbling outwardly.
Silent screaming inwardly.

So much happens when my hands are in water.

Water is a conduit for much as everything is energy and water transfers that energy.

For me, typically water gives me *ideas* and *characters to write, stories to tell,* and *awareness* around something that's being processed.

Well, I was wrist-deep
in a shit-ton of awareness
and I was choosing to be unhappy about it all.

Catch that—*to be unhappy in a moment is nothing more than a choice.*

The dish soap that came with the place was vivid blue.

Something I'd never buy and typically would not use, but we had just arrived and this was our very first night together.

And first fight. *Again.*

His voice soft. *Unsure.* Struggling to understand.
My voice loud. *Harsh.* Feeling angry and unheard.

This damn soap,
so strong,
overpowering me,
much like my *over-the-top* emotions.

I remember this putrid chemical odor surrounding us like a thick, too-fragrant cloud.

My body, senses, intolerant to most chemicals.
Much like I was being that evening.

So I'm arguing with the husband and the smell of the
detergent *permeates the entire conversation*.

We go through the highs and lows—*the disconnect*—
forever *misunderstanding*.

Sighs (on my part),
Head shakes (on his).

Tears (on my end),
Pleading looks (on his).

Lack of *connection*.
Incapable of *understanding*.

All the emotional overload
Bubble-wrapped in sudsy chemicals.

Dishes, half-washed, *forgotten*.

The argument, eventually, brushed away,
never forgotten.

But worked through
like so much
these last few years.

Acceptance.
Allowing.
My new middle names—
competing, of course, with more JOY.

Pass the detachment, pretty please.

And then years later,
from this new state of being,
where JOY is my default setting,
I find myself squirting a stream of blue on a sponge,
the only option at hand.

And immediately, shockingly, I'm transported
through time.

Hands once again sinking in doing the—*shout it out, yo—*
Frigging dishes!

The smell, which lived within my memory banks
on a cellular level,
took me right back to
that *night*,
that *fight*.

All of a sudden I was angry.
Fuming mad.

Steam arising from the hot water
and my scalding temper.

The glass in my hand, in serious jeopardy of a good
old tossing.

I didn't, but man, upon occasion, I so want to . . .

To break the tension erupting within me.
To hear the shattering of glass,
of something, anything
but me.

If you please.

Because even though that
misunderstanding, disagreement, argument
was now years in my rearview mirror . . .

it was a good thing The Frenchman
wasn't present in that new moment
as he could have been in the crosshairs of my

—welcome back—

short-tempered,
emotional
everloaded
fuse.

Brought to the surface
by *sensory* memory.

Crazy, no?

energy in motion

Emotions are energy in motion.

Think about that for a moment.
When we shut down our emotions,
they become trapped in the body
as motion must go somewhere.

Emotions like sadness, fear, anger, or pain—
once trapped in our bodies,
these can make us physically ill.

This is what I now know happened to me at age
twelve.

I stuffed all the pain of a happily unhappy childhood
inside.

I suddenly became cold, *painfully so.*

I started to gain weight, 20 pounds in a year.

Then more.

Ah, teenagers. Moody little shits.
That was the consensus.

Yet I had stuffed so many emotions
my entire childhood
without a safe outlet.

Believing a story of being *seen not heard.*

With no one to talk to
even if I *could* or *would* speak—
given that story I held tight to.

Seen but not heard.

A security blanket suffocating me
even as it protected who I thought I *should* be . . .

Instead, forever spinning in my analytical brain,
thoughts that never stopped questioning—
asking *why this, why that* on repeat . . .

Working so diligently to process
that which I had no programming for,
no known-to-me definitions from which to define . . .

Struggling *solo* to create a foundation to work from . . .

With no point of understanding,
of reference.

No anchor to grab on to.
No words to communicate my needs.

Forever treading water,
tossed about in a rough,
winter-gray sea . . .

Never realizing
all I needed to do
was place my feet
on the solid ground beneath me . . .

And allow the *thigh*-high waters to rush on by—
no need to drown me . . .

Never once understanding
until my forties
that I was fully supported,
always.

All the blame and shame.
All the self-loathing.
All the hate.
All the anger and pain,
sadness, and misery.

Left unexpressed,
it all landed in my gut,
ill will spreading . . .

Feeding my *unhappy*,
my *dis*-ease of being me.

Enabling me to swim in stories of . . .

The world is out to get me.
My body betrayed me.
The second shoe always drops.

I'm broken.

weight

For years, I believed I was sick.

I carried that dis-*ease of me* around like a *cross to bear*, and it became a *physical* weight.

It started in my teens and exploded in my twenties.

I'm barely 5 feet 2 inches (157 centimeters) and weighed in at 299.5 pounds (roughly 136 kilograms) in my mid-twenties.

I was drowning in self-hate.
Until at twenty-eight . . .

I flipped a switch
in one desperate moment
and chose a new fate.

A new way of being,
of showing up for me.

This started my two-year journey,
shedding 180 pounds,
an ushering in of the *real* me
less all that toxicity.

Each pound was a *story* I *chose* to shed.

Hear that *loud* and *clear*.

If you've got a tummy that won't disappear,
feel you have fat thighs,
hate the shape of your chinny-chin-chin . . .

Story.
Story.
Story.

Let
each
one
go.

And the weight will melt
away.

But not if you keep a story of
self-hate.

For me it was saying adios to
one story at a time.

Until, 180 stories,
pounds,
were no longer mine
to own,
to be weighed down by,
to carry around.

Consider looking at what stories are keeping you from living your most delicious life.

A life of JOY,
of peace,
of intention,
of purpose.

Imagine pulling the threads of your beliefs—
about yourself, your life, the world around you—
and you will uncover stories.

The question is,

Once you see them, do you choose to keep owning them if they no longer serve you, or do you choose to cut them loose?

Food for scrumptious thought.

spun to undone

I spun stories for twenty years; I was a pro at spinning.

I spun the story of my childhood,
the story that I was *too loud,*
the story that I had to be the *good girl,*
that I wasn't enough,
and so many others . . .

Most of them a sticky trap lining the way to self-
sabotage.

I spun them and pushed them down, and then I spun
them again.

I remember the Bio Mom walking me into school
one day.

I was in the second grade with strawberry blonde hair
forever pulled into a tight ponytail—at least for the
start of my day.

We were stopped by my teacher,
a woman who smiled more than both my first grade
teachers combined.

I can still see their shoes.
Shiny pairs of black high heels.
One pair of legs encased in nude-colored pantyhose,
the other tinted a strange tan.

I remember thinking, clear as day, *I'm never gonna wear those gross pantyhose.*

And I never did. *Pantyhose. Just yuck!*

But what came next is the point of this *story*-share.

Suddenly, my attention caught on the words my teacher stated with conviction, "Jill's bad in math."

I remember looking up, thinking the Bio Mom might stand up for me. I mean that's what moms do after all, *is it not?*

Instead, she nodded. "Yes, Jill's bad at math."

In that moment, I had a choice.

Accept that story as my own and believe it or reject it.

I accepted that story.

My choice,
as I was a child,
looking up at two adults.

Two women who were supposed to *know best*,
whose job it was to support me,
or so I thought.

And so I *became* bad at math.
Full stop.

Until that point, I had struggled.

Just as I struggled to read, focus, comprehend.
Placed in special ed.

But in that moment, that agreement,
I gave all my power away and picked up the torch that
burned oh-so bright for decades on end.

Jill is bad in math.

I carried that shit *almost* proudly.

curious kitty

This makes me curious.

No longer sad or mad,
tossing my hands up in
a *why me?*
moment of pity,
of despair . . .

As how many other stories
did I unknowingly
receive,
accept,
own as my own,
and believe
wholeheartedly.

Makes you take a beat and say "hmmm," does it not?

This story—*Jill's bad in math*—shaped so much,
brought so much misery
and so much *opportunity*.

There are *always* two sides to the same coin.
More on that to come.

This story was one handed to me by those I was
taught to respect.

That one story set the trajectory for so much of my life

the *positive* and *negative* effects impossible to ignore.

Confirming there is never a *wrong* step taken in this thing called life.
Only a step not taken.

Get curious about your stories and leave *the why me mentality* duct taped, hogtied, and in the truck of someone else's abandoned car.

the undoing

It was in my freshman year of college, sitting in the nosebleed section of college algebra, when something shifted, and I no longer had to dread being a failure, *yet again*, in math.

The monotone voice of the teaching assistant—this class didn't rate high enough for a professor to teach it—was busy working out a problem on the overhead projector.

Bored out of my mind, listening to him drone on as his larger-than-life hand solved the problem step-by-step, I saw this was going to take time.

To say he was slow was an understatement.

So I wrote the problem at the top of my notebook, and much like a doodle in the margins, started to work it out.

Giving it *no weight, no thought, no attention.*

Just one step, then the next step . . . *emotionlessly, automatically.*

This was back in the day, when you had to show all your work, because that's how one learned math.

*Oh how delicious it is to age myself like a fine,
French wine.*

I didn't *think* about getting it *right*.
I didn't *worry* about getting it *wrong*.

I just did the steps, tuning out his nasal voice as it filled
the space around me.

I circled my answer. *Done.*

Not attached to the rightness of my answer because
my story screamed internally, *Jill's bad in math . . .*

Not expecting a thing, I looked up, tempted to check
the clock on the wall behind me but afraid only a
handful of seconds of this ninety-minute class
had passed.

This was hell.

Suddenly, I saw him circle his answer, the slow-ass TA.

And bored, I checked what I had circled against his
neater scrawl—*I'll give him that*—and saw it *matched*.

His answer.
My answer.
One and the—*what?!*—same.

**Without thought,
no stress,
with total ease,
I had solved a math problem.**

And at first I thought . . .
Naaah! Please!

How quick I was to dismiss a win.

How quick to not believe goodness within.
Interesting, is it not?

A girl next to me leaned over and punched me in the arm. "You got it right? Do it again. Show me what you did."

I watched her hair all but bounce in delicious synchronicity as she nodded at my paper. I flipped the page over and wrote out the problem on a fresh sheet. Slowly, I worked it out, showing her exactly what I did.

Step-by-step till I circled my answer yet again.

She looked at my paper.
She looked at the professor's work.
She grinned back at me. "You got it right again."

Well, hot damn. I did. Right *again*.

She hit a cute guy on the other side of her and told him, "Look at her. She's smart." She pointed at me. "Do it again."

I did it again, face beet red. *Smart? In math?*
Insert mental snort.

Third time's a charm. Damn, I like things three by three.

Cute Guy leaned past the girl with the massive Afro. "I'm sitting next to you more often."

And in that moment, I realized I had a new choice, a new story to accept.

I could do math.

Granted, I'd gotten a single problem right—
times three.

There is so much to be said for threes—
for me.

I could pooh-pooh that event and blow it off as *nothingness*

or sink in with a delighted shiver, quiver
and see endless *possibilities*.

I remember flipping the page in my notebook, glancing up and going for it again.

New problem
written at the top of my page.

Carefully checked to confirm no numbers
had been flipped.
I was, after all, a pro at that.

And as the Monotone Guy worked through the problem at a snail's pace, I put my head down and found a solution.

Not only was I done first, but I was impatient to see if my circled answer was what he too got at the end of his spiel.

Leaning forward, I remember squinting as he completed his circle, marking the problem complete.

A check once, twice, *damn girl—You can do math.*

And in that moment, as JOY became a tingle mixed with pride, I celebrated with a booty dance in my mind's eye.

Shake-shaking to my own steady beat.
I can do math.
New story told.
New way of being now *able to unfold.*

It's as simple as that.
As complex as all that.

Like all things, it's a *choice* to believe a story.

When you see that,
get that,
own that,
you now can change all.

And in that moment I did.

My new story bloomed within.

I can do math. Booyah, bitches!

why way

Was the first story a lie?

I could have chosen to go down the rabbit hole of
Why? Why? Why?

But instead, I chose to focus on this new heady feeling
of *I Can* because in that moment I saw the truth.

The truth is—

Why doesn't matter.

Consider where the *why* often leads.
Down *Victim* Avenue.

A crossroads of more *Why Ways* to explore,
become lost in.

Because each *why* asked
leads to a maze of
ten, a hundred more.

A never-ending loop,
a thousand more dips, turns, bends
to questions that take one farther away from
the *win*, the *point*, that which *is* the sole focus,
should one desire to stay the course of one's *truth*.

And change a story, shot down for good.

A rather simple focus in this moment—
now, present in that College Algebra class—

I can do math.

Mic-drop moment. Enough said.

labels

In the same year of college, I was tested for dyslexia.

Even though I'd worked my way into the honor's program. A way to create my most delicious schedule ahead of all the other students and have access to smaller classes—not common, nosebleed section, packed ones.

One literature professor, in a class of twenty, saw something in me that caught his eye.
So I took the test.

A thing I despised, but this one didn't *count*.
No harm. No foul. No seed of doubt.

But this test did, in fact, count big-time
as a title was given.

Dyslexic was I.

And in that moment, I realized,
Ooh, labels. I really don't like labels.
Reject. Reject. Reject.

If you remember, I'd been placed in *special ed*, back in elementary school. During a time there was nothing *special* about it.

And I made a choice to not accept this new story.
To not buy into what I could have taken as a crutch.

My personal excuse sword.
Dyslexic Diva.

I was, after all, good at that.
Excuses. Roles. Victimhood.

I'd played the part of *Teacher's Pet.*

I knew how to *manipulate* the system so I could
hide . . .

I understood the path of *Excuse*ville firsthand
and willingly had a 24/7 love affair with it.

But new school,
new state,
new me.

I chose differently.

Everything is a choice.

story-web weaving

Without a way to cut ourselves free from stories, we spin them forever, even if we reject them. We become trapped in the web we have spun for ourselves.

If there's one thing to take away from these pages, it's that *everything is a story.*

What story are you telling yourself right now?

That this feels *hard*?
Don't know where to even *begin*?

Press pause and realize those are stories too.
Stories that show up for you again and again.

Just sink into this moment,
these words
and allow what comes next to unfold.

Consider in this moment . . .

What story or judgement are you spinning about me, the one shining a spotlight on some hard-hitting truth?

It's okay. Judge away. Simply know this truth:

That which you judge in another you are judging in yourself as well.

fire ants

You are *supported* in all things.

When you know this
on a soul-deep level,
your actions shift,
your stories change

And your very life *evolves*
into one you may have never imagined possible—
until now.

Take me as an example.
Let's consider where I am right now.

Living my most delicious life.

A little cottage
on a hill,
surrounded by secret gardens—

currently in the works—
overlooking the sea,
where I sit all day and write.

That was but a childhood dream,
a dream I never gave any thought to owning,
to making my reality.

Until I got out of my own way.
Until I found my voice.
Until I decided I was *worthy* enough.

And it took another, my Frenchman, to set the ball in motion, to alert me to the fact that *I am enough* to own, live, rock any dream I so desire.

What aren't you allowing to be possible in your own stories of limitation?

Tales of lack . . .
Fear of not being good enough . . .
Doubt? Procrastination . . .

The limiting stories
we tell over and over again
that keep us stuck,
an endless trail down a back-assward path of you.

When you tap into *what you hold dear, what you value*, you will shed those stories like you would a stream of fire ants that found their way up your leg.

You'll be stomping and shaking those stories off for dear life.

Feeling that sting,
that bite,
the heat.

This is what most stories—
believed, owned, and told on repeat,
do to us
day in,
day out.

We are simply
so accustomed,
so used to, the pain
it's become absurdly comfortable.

Let go of those stories
that suck your very life force,
stealing your essence, your dreams, your very energy,
worse than a single ant on fire.

a secret affair

I kept my writing secret for a long time. And in turn I kept who I was hidden.

I published my first article when I was seventeen—in a leading men's magazine.

And yeah, I lied about my age. The *good girl* side of me felt guilty about that for more than thirty years.

Yet, the *bad girl*, slightly naughty side of me, enjoyed that lie and kept it alive.

That delicious, slightly addictive feeling of having a secret all mine to own.

That was something I *hugged close* and *held onto like a comfy sweater,* for nearly three decades. *Protected*.

Until recently, I never personally shared my writing with anyone.

Not my family. Not The Frenchman.

It was simply mine to own. To snuggle up with, to giggle about, and to keep insanely private.

But like too much of anything dark, delicious, and decadently binge-worthy, my secret affair left me solo, on my own.

A story-sage of isolation, of not seen nor heard. Told now by little old me. No longer another.

There is no sharing of wins, no celebrating moments. Instead, there is a warm rush of *wham-bam-thank-you-ma'am.*

And I kinda liked that.

Hiding in plain sight. Snickering at my own dirty, little secret.

In fact, I fed off it.

But the downside of my closeted way of being was I didn't enJOY the *writer is me* moments.

I made praise and accolades so unimportant as to be nonexistent.

And I got to remain hidden, *safe.*

Comfortable even. Because praise, that shit freaked me out.

So instead of being uncomfortable, stepping out

Instead of allowing rejection, praise, criticism, respect, judgement to be experienced

Instead of sinking into the support, love, praise and reaping the rewards of the impact I was making . . .

I chose to remain alone in the bubble of me.

Writing *happily*. Creating *easily*. Shrink-wrapped *protectively*.

Unconcerned if another was judging me.
Uncaring if my words touched someone's soul.

Yet, is that really the true-blue me?

Hell no, I'm *a too-sensitive soul*, if I listen to one story of my past.

Hell no, *I love people*, if I really tap into my deep-down needs.

A crushing, unfulfilled desire to help others succeed.

My purple-penned words were either for me and me alone or hidden behind another name, *ghosted* for another or *an alter ego* I chose to write under.

And I loved it as I got to focus on the craft, the words, the work.

And I got to protect all my limiting stories.

Catch that as it's what we delightful humans do.

We create stories to support the stories we aren't ready to let go of.

Hell, I created characters, contracts . . . worlds to protect my delicious secret.

Only my agent/editor knows all my hidden nooks

and writing crannies, as we've now been together for years and years—more enmeshed than most married couples I know.

And it worked, but *internally*, a part of me made it *wrong* . . .

Gave *hiding in plain sight* a story of being *broken*, when in fact, it allowed me to *flourish* and *share* stories with hundreds, thousands, possibly millions of souls.

There are always two sides to every *story*-coin.

And that is the power of story . . . the stories we tell ourselves.

The stories we keep alive.

The ones we bake in as it's more comfortable than not to.

Stories impact us,
keep us trapped, stuck . . .

While others allow us to soar.

The type of story you tell, once newly aware, is up to you.

And that's *delicious* news.

silence

When I introduced silence into my life, the ground under me shifted. Because I finally took time to get to know me.

To see that staying in my busy, my overdoing-ness was actually keeping me from getting to know me.

Because point-blank, *I didn't like me.*

And silence scared me. Made all the thoughts I'd gotten so good at ignoring, stuffing, denying bubble up to the surface of me.

The stories *of less than, fraud, fake, lacking, broken, needing to be fixed*, and most of the time completely *unlovable*.

Unlovable because honestly, I hated me.

How else could I ever answer my Frenchman's most pressing question the last few years when I was so sad, so emotionally high-strung, so lost.

What do you even want, Jill?

Silence showed me much,
but getting to a space,
where I felt comfortable

with the silence,
that took grace.

I gave myself a gift of doing nothing but *being* and
saw that I hardly ever took time to process *wins,
accomplishments, conversations.*

To process my day.

In the silence, *I found my voice*. Funny how that works.

I discovered what I want
and what I don't.

I listened to *me*.

The truth is, when you learn to listen to yourself, *all*
opens to you, *for* you.

If you want to start living new stories, I invite you to
spend time getting to know your true self.

And if it scares the crap out of you
to sit quietly alone and do nothing,
perfect.

Get *un*comfortable with your fine self.

And if it's a breeze
to be,
to do nothing,
to just hear your thoughts.
Perfect.

No judgement here or there.

Allow the minutes to tick by
one by one,
then see what *magic* comes.

Because it's in *this* space
where truth,
your truth,
lies.

Where that *hell yeah* voice resides.

The inner knowing that all seek
but don't know how to claim.

It starts with practicing *nothingness*
like it's a *game*.

Buckle up because it's time to get *comfortable* with
being *uncomfortable*.

Purple Pen
PRACTICE

sink into thirty-three minutes of silence today

When my mentor suggested four hours of silence, my jaw literally hit the floor.

I'm not going to even suggest you do that, as that's *his* thing, and I'll share more about him later on.

What I am going to say is this . . .

If you want to tap into the stories within,
all the tales spinning and swirling,
holding you hostage, *stuck*
in overthinking mode

If you've ever wanted to stop those replaying convos,
the ones you have on repeat over and over again in
your head

If you're here, in these pages, searching for answers,
it's my role right now to tell you the most fabulous,
scary truth.

The answers you seek on

how to decode you,
how to live a better life,
how to let go of the pain,
how to finally fucking succeed,

how to know what you really want,
they all lie *within* you.

Within the silence. There for you to access at any time.

And that's good news.
You are both the *lock* and the *key*
to the most delicious you.

Silence is literally your soon-to-be best friend.

When you sink in.

Because the silence doesn't lie.

It's like the brightest flashlight burning high.
A beam you get to direct deep within
and see clearly what's been hiding,
laying in wait.

Give yourself the gift of just thirty-three minutes
within the next twenty-four hours.

Book it, baby, and soon you will be floored at just
what comes to the surface of you.

When ready, sink into your favorite chair,
sit in the lush green grass of your yard,
be present in a place where no one can barge in,
no partner can ask you a question,
no little ones can demand a snack pack.

This is a time for you.

Nothing but
me, myself, and I.

Silence your phone.
Silence your mind.

Sounds simple, right?

Yet this is where it gets hard for so many of us.
Where it became hard for me.

If you feel the need to fidget,
don't judge it.

Just acknowledge and allow it to fade away.

If you feel the need to feel something—*anything*—
good. Do.

Anger, sadness, tears, a snort-laugh.

Have at it and allow it,
the feelings, to slip out,
to slide away.

Don't stop the tears, the smile, the desire to focus on a
thought.

Allow it all.

Simply pay attention to what comes up for you.
What thoughts come in,
what convos you replay,
what list of to-dos you start alphabetizing . . .

And as each *thought, need, desire to move*
enters your consciousness . . .

Give it a mental wave,
a nonverbal *thank-you*,
and allow it to flow on by.

And those emotions, simply name them as they
rumble up and tumble out.

When thirty-three minutes is at an end, consider
jotting down a few notes on what you feel in that
moment.

What came up for you?

And this is key—
know that you did it all *perfectly*.

If nothing came to the surface, *good*.

If all kinds of monkeys started a heavy metal band of
head-chatter, *good*.

There is no right and no wrong way here.
It's a story to believe there is.

Feel daring?

Schedule your next thirty-three minutes of silence to
take place within the next twenty-four hours or less.

Getting *good* at silence is like getting good at anything—

Repetition is the mother of all skill.

And yes, before you begin, set an alarm—a gentle bell or soft chimes that will alert you when it's time—but do put that phone away . . .

In your bag, upside down and just out of reach.

This is truly a *disconnecting from all* so you can *reconnect with who you are* and *discover who you desire to become.*

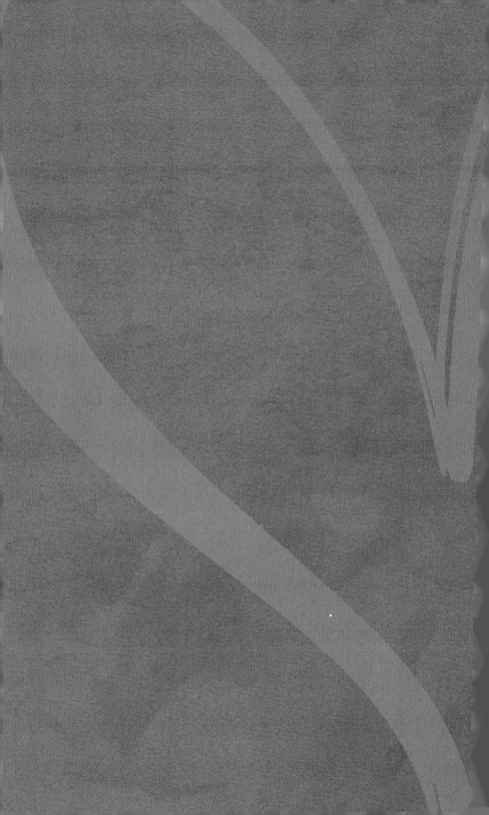

3: The Stories You Tell Yourself

The Stories You Tell Yourself

Facts tell, stories *sell*.
And that is the truth.

What stories are you selling?

Yourself . . .
Others . . .

In the daylight . . .
In the dead of night . . . ?

stories are everywhere

We learn through stories. Way before we had written words on a page, we passed down our stories through folklore.

We sat around campfires
or a cauldron . . .

Listening to elders, those with something to say, learning through . . . *stories*.

And we told stories.

This is how people discovered the world they lived in, saw how the community or hierarchy worked, and uncovered ways of being for themselves.

We heard stories, absorbed stories—often without question.

We learned to tell stories.

Some that served, others that did not.

Think about how many stories live *inside* you right now.

You have access to the most incredible computer on the planet.

And it's within you.

We start with *very little programming* as infants.

In fact, imagine for a moment you came into the world empty.

A blank, *eager* slate.

Consider that you, at one time, not only had adorable baby fat but also an empty *hard-drive* brain, free of all but the *basic* functionality software.

Those programs that kept you *breathing, sucking, eliminating, growing* as you *absorbed* all around you, *a curious little sponge.*

Every system, or *hard drive*, needs rules, guidelines to follow.

In the computer world, these are called *programs*.

As an infant and even as a child, you're in *record mode* 24/7.

Just taking in data.
Absorbing stories.

Sitting around that proverbial campfire, hanging on tall tales and truthful ones with utter delight, captivated as though they are warm, sticky marshmallows, gooey from roasting over that open flame of drama.

Because let's get honest for a hot sec.

Most stories contain an element or two of the

dramatic. That thing that tugs on your heartstrings, gets your blood boiling, increases your heartbeat, steals your breath, or has the hairs on the back of your neck standing at attention.

That drama, that response, is exactly what reels us in. *Hook. Line. And sinker.*

We get stories from our family, our teachers, our community, the media, friends, literature, movies, the music we turn up high.

Everything, all of these stories, from a very early age, are *recorded* and *stored* and become part of your *sub*conscious programming.

Much like *breathing*, these stories often become *beliefs* or *truths* that then run on *the autopilot of you* . . . in your background, *without thought.*

So imagine yourself for a moment, a wee lad or lass, rolling around gleefully in your *happy-baby* pose. A little ray of JOY, *observing* and *absorbing* everything, with curious wonder, even delight and *not a single filter* yet in sight.

We don't censor, question, or even understand most of what comes in during these very early years.

We simply are a conduit *receiving*, *allowing*, and *inviting* all in—JOYfully.

There is nothing to understand.

No judgements made about the *quality* of stories nor the programming absorbed.

No asking whether this new data is *good* or *bad*, serves us or does not serve us.

It, *all of it*, simply becomes part of you—part of *your story*.

#truth

So what stories are you telling yourself and, without question, believing as your truth?

There are the stories *we tell ourselves.*

The stories *we tell others about ourselves.*

The stories *others tell us about ourselves.*

And stories *the world tells us about ourselves.*

To sum it up, that's a hell of a lot of *fiction* we marinate in on the daily.

Believing,
in our flawed—*perhaps*
thinking,
that all of it,
any of it
is . . .

Real.
True.
Absolute.

simply impactful

Many of our stories are simple:

good girl,
bad girl,
black sheep,
tomboy
entitled one.

But the impact they can have
can be the *Gorilla Glue*
that keeps us stuck, stuck—
damn-it-that-shit's-strong
stuck.

Once you own a story,
any story,
the next step taken—*automatically*—
is to align or not to align.

So often done without thought.

Yet when you're ready,
it's time to stop spinning
in your web of disempowering tales
and start a-cutting.

This *can* be fun. If you *say* it is.

forget fun

I'm a good girl—so I do this, I don't do that.

I can't tell you how much fun I *refused* to take part
in throughout my life because I was a *good girl, a
people-pleaser, a worrier.*

The designated driver,
designated controller of everything.

No parties *enjoyed*,
no dance clubs *pulsed*,
no rolls in the proverbial hay.

Tinder me what? No fucking way.

No jump-from-great-heights
daredevil me.

It's always been my job, instead, to save the proverbial
day.

Ah, the weight of it all becoming heavier and heavier,
a noose wrapped tight around my dainty neck.

A slipknot no one ever asked me to tie.

All stories, *identities*
I picked up

and owned as pieces of me
from a very early age.

Taken,
learned,
absorbed
from fairy tales, the media,
parents, family, friends . . .

If we learn to see our stories for what they are—
choices, decisions made

that, if they no longer serve,
we can now change—

there is *freedom* to be found.

And the *possibility* to create a most delicious life.

reject, eject

What stories are you carrying that are old and tired?

What stories no longer serve the *you* you want to become?

What stories do you hang on to,
like nails digging in for dear life
to the Cliff of You?

A rejection of what is, what one believes . . .

Now that is the secret sauce to spice up your life,
to change your state,
to begin the creation of a most delicious life.

What does that mean, to *reject a story*?

To let go of an identity that no longer serves you?
To say *adios* to a belief you no longer need?

I'm always amazed at how willing I once was
to white-knuckle grip those stories that hurt me,
even once I recognized them.

How deeply ingrained the need was to refuse to let them go,
even knowing they are not mine to own.

To do so would have been ejecting myself willingly
from the G5 speed of my fighter-pilot life . . .

Even seeing when a story didn't serve me but pushed
me under the tide,
spun me into a nosedive.

Because they came entrenched in
what I should do,
who I should be,
how I should act,
what I should say, do, think, feel.

If you can relate,
do not debate the wasted years,
the depressed state
that tempts to consume you.

Instead, *acknowledge* and *allow* yourself to *let go.*

To do this requires forgiveness of self,
no longer picking up the stick of self-hatred,
beating yourself black and blue.

Instead, what's possible
if you are *grateful* for this moment of clarity,
of awakening,
of awareness,
and allow what you feel
to ebb and flow.

A deep, natural breath
in and out.

I know;
I've been there,
done that for years, decades . . .

Retelling the same old story,
the one that made me feel *sick, angry, hurt*.

Much like my hands sinking into the dishes yet again,
the story of a past argument with The Frenchman
suddenly burning hot, front and center

spinning

spinning

spinning

Me once again.

sharing is caring

While men and women speak close to the same number of words daily . . .

It's actually false to say that women talk more than men, which used to be considered *fact*, funny enough, and turns out is just another—say it with me—*story!*

Men do tend to use their words very differently than the opposite sex.

No joke. This is science, *yo*.

Women share. We are, generally speaking, communicators and storytellers.

We *bond* over stories.
We *comfort* with stories.
We *educate* through stories.
We *case-build* by retelling stories.

Storytelling is not positive or negative. It simply is.

The stories we spin, however, ask yourself:

Do they serve me or do they keep me stuck?

conversations

It's Friday girls' night.
Look mama, no kids.

Saturday afternoon book club.
More your cup of tea?

Maybe it's Sunday brunch
Or that yoga time
followed by a green smoothie
with a friend or two.

At one point, more often than not, the conversation
turns to *shared* stories.

And can turn quickly to commiserating,
feeling each other's pain.

Imagine conversations you yourself have taken part in.
How often have they taken a turn into something like

I can't lose this weight no matter what I do . . .

*I hate my hips, my thighs. See these underarms, they
wave bye-bye.*

Swimsuit shopping, so god-awful.

My husband this . . .

My marriage that . . .

OMG, the kids are driving me crazy . . .

Another flipping laugh line. Look at me, girls, I don't even laugh anymore!

I don't know where I fit in anymore. What I even want.

Where did my zest for life, my passion, go?

We often spin negative stories together.
In disjoined harmony.

Misery loves company.

And this plants seeds.

These stories, *if allowed in*, can take root within you, can add to the stories you already own that fester like fast-growing weeds just below the surface of your soil.

And once root is taken, those seeds can bloom into fresh doubt, sprouting new tales left unsaid. To marinate, to soak, to consume you.

Those stories you never tell a soul but that are on repeat in your head each and every night.

The worry you have over your husband's wandering eye.

The fact that you haven't had sex in over a month.

Is he seeing someone else?

153

The thought that maybe he doesn't love you.

The story that maybe you're no longer enough.

Does this sound familiar?

It can be flipped the other way.

> *I have to all but beg for it.*
> *And even then, it's like she's put off by me.*
> *Does she no longer love me?*
> *She used to crave my touch, enjoy my attention.*
> *And now, she doesn't want to touch me?*
> *No longer wants me to touch her . . .*
> *What did I do wrong?*
> *Maybe she no longer finds me good looking . . .*

Believe you me, men also swim in untold stories that play round and round in their own head.

One seed can quickly become a garden of strangling weeds that cast shadows, stretching and reaching and snuffing out any possibility.

A fabulous mentor of mine often says, "What's most vulnerable is most general."

Ah, how very, very true.

Meaning, if you're having thoughts and start thinking, *What I'm going through is so very personal, I can't possibly share.*

Chances are ten other people in a room of twelve are having similar thoughts and feelings.

Many are going through those exact ups and downs,
feeling as alone,
slipping silently under the heavy waves of it all,
just as you are doing.

And that's why I'm writing about topics most will sweep under the rug.

That's why I'm pulling back the curtain
and shining a bright light
on that which makes even me
most uncomfortable.

Cheers to going from hiding in plain sight, to standing on the stage of what's most taboo.

Yet I'm willing to expose myself, to be real,
to be seen . . .

Because the real crime is to remain *in* the story.
In the lie of believing you are the *only* one.
Oh-so alone.

It's time to stop the spin.

End believing in that very story
that keeps you trapped.

Are you in?

fucking salad

To sink this home, let me paint a little visual story.

A handful of women go to Sunday brunch.

One woman orders a salad and makes a comment about *trying to lose weight.*

The conversation quickly centers around which parts of the women's bodies they are unhappy with or want to change.

I can't seem to let go of this baby weight. I feel so fat.

Well, I haven't had a baby in more than a decade and that ten pounds, girl, it's not yet found another zip code. Good luck with that.

Oh, I simply have no time. Gym? Please. I got three kids. Well, four if you count that husband of mine.

I hear you. My husband told me my ass was fat just last week. I swear if I didn't have his babies, I'd wanna . . .

What? Leave him? I think about my escape plan every day when I'm not thinking about how none of my clothes fit.

I think I have a double chin.

Fucking salad. I hate salad. Who wants a cheeseburger? Fries?

Suddenly this group of women is engaged in a *shaming* of their own bodies, relationships, lives, themselves, which serves none.

When we spin stories *with* others, we are *accepting* their energy. We are adding *their* energy to *our* story.

Because I'll say it again: *everything is energy.*

This can be great if the conversation is positive and present tense.

Look at your conversations . . .

Those with yourself,
your girlfriends.

Do they raise you up or sink you low?

justified

Often, though, sharing with others or listening to another's tale leaves us feeling demotivated about change or justified in our decisions to stay the same.

So let's dive into this little nugget my own coach shared with me.

It's called case-building, and it's what we do, men and women, when we go looking for *examples, confirmation, agreement outside oneself* to support our stories.

As human beings we so crave community.

We *want* to belong.

I'd dare to say we *need* to belong on some level.

We want to feel *loved.*
We need to feel *supported.*
We desire to feel *heard.*

This is why we once gathered around campfires and listened to the elders share their folklore.

Yet with community comes many pros and cons, like with all things in life. There are always two sides of the same *idea* coin.

The tendency is to share the stories we need *validated* in that community.

The pitfall is looking for
permission,
approval,
the steps toward a goal,
feedback on a relationship . . .

From that group, that community,
from outside ourselves.

When you open yourself up this way and allow others to put their spin, their thoughts, their energy into your stories, that right there is the moment you can lose yourself.

Disconnecting from your own inner knowing, believing others' opinions to be as important, if not more important, than your own . . .

Belonging to a community, such as a family, a workplace, a church, a book club, a neighborhood, a country . . .

These add to your life or rob you of your most delicious future.

Who are you . . .

without your name,
without your culture,
without your profession . . . ?

The choice is yours to pay attention to what others in all the arenas of your life say, think, and feel about you

Or start tapping into what you want to *say, think, believe*, and *feel* about yourself.

bossy

I was *bossy*. And rather proud of it.
Not seeing all the *layers* of that one five-letter word.

Look at the *connotation* of that word.

Bossy.

It's rather negative, is it not?
Demeaning in a way.

Rarely is it applied to a male, at least not in my world.

Yet *assertive* . . . now that *feels* different.

Even looking up the two words online is *telling*.

"Don't be so *bossy*."—as though it's a bad thing . . .

Ah, hello, judgement.

"This job may call for *assertive* behavior."—simply a
way of being . . .

I now *choose* to *not* be seen as bossy,
for the most part,
as it's still a running family joke.

But in business, no longer am I that.

In contract negotiations,
book deals,
working with A-listers to write their words,
assertive is me.

With my Frenchman, I to aligned.

To me simply being me.

I now know what I want.
And I'm no longer afraid to speak up.

Nothing *bossy* in that now is there?

If another chooses to see me
finding my voice, owning my words,
telling my story my way
as *bossy*,
that is their interpretation . . .

And it has *nothing* to do with me.

Catch that golden word-nugget as you can take it to
the bank that will fund your most delicious life.

How someone sees you,
what they say about you,
that's on them,
not you.

When you get solid with you. . .

When you tap into the truth that another's opinion of you is more about themselves than you . . .

you will be free.

Both words create a *story* of who I can be.
Bossy. Assertive.

Who I believe others see me as being.
That's on them and is none of my business.

I allow words to *define* me.
Or not.

Stories, I *create* to shape me.
Or not.

Those *created about me*
to *become* me.
Or not.

And the funny thing is, I have no clue where *bossy is me*—the story—first began.

Probably not even as a story created by me,
as I'm sure one day I didn't wake up and say,
bossy is me.

I most likely heard it said about me.
Just like *Jill is bad in math*.
And allowed it in.

Received that word as my new truth,
an addition to the story of me.

**Take a moment now and consider a story
or just one word that you said to yourself or
another said to you.**

A story or word, you have *accepted,* consciously or
not, that has shaped who you are today.

Jot it down in your own delicious journal.

Lean in and *feel* into those one, two, or three word(s)
you used to *describe* you.

The story you choose to *own* about you.

For me, the difference between *bossy* and *assertive* is
night and day.

The *bossy* wife or the *assertive* wife.
Paints two very different pictures in my mind.

The *bossy* CEO and the *assertive* CEO.

If you are a female CEO, there is a difference in how
you perceive and carry yourself; is there not?

What others choose to see you as is none of your
concern.

How you choose to see yourself, that is everything.

That is the *you* who shows up in the world.

hard

We make things so damn hard for ourselves, do we not?

I know I sure did. Here's what I know now.

That is a story, a way of being—*needing to make things hard.*

Now you get to decide:

Does that way of showing up in life, making it all so damn hard, serve me?

If no, let it go and dive into a new way . . .

If yes, all righty then.

No more complaining, no blaming, no shaming. *Choice made.*

Stories give us our place in the world.

Isn't it about time you penned a tale that served you, empowered you?

Imagine if you took up space,
not the *people-pleasing corner,*
the victim-is-me wall,
the martyrdom spin—within.

Whatever the story you've been cast in,
took up the torch
and carried—
so faithfully,
so diligently.

You can now choose to let it go.

What if now you get to be 100 percent responsible?

That was a sore spot for me, accepting responsibility for the crap stories handed to me.

To own my role in the choice of my *retelling, owning, forever sinking into*, and *allowing* a story, any story, to become a part of who I decided to be.

But in this sudden sucky awareness that I am responsible for keeping or rejecting a story, for spinning in it or tossing it aside . . .

In that, came a magical moment of utter divineness.

I could choose to tell a new tale at any moment.

You get to tell whatever story you want.

If you don't like your story anymore

acknowledge it,
recognize it,
and then *change it.*

Let the old story go . . .

Without making it wrong.
Without making you bad, bad, bad
to the bone.

That is key.

If you make it more complicated than that, look
at your life and see where else you overanalyze.
Overcomplicate.

Dramatize.

Tend to blame and shame yourself.
Or another.

Boy oh boy, that was once me.
Draining way of being.

When you choose to say ah, hell no to stories that
press you down, you make room for a new story to
bloom.

When you choose only stories that fill you
with JOY,
with purpose . . .

When you choose new stories
that support you . . .

the weight, so heavy upon your shoulders, eases.

And—yes!—that's when you are creating your most
delicious life.

forgive

What if the path to your most delicious life,
is to let it all go.

To shed the layers of you that no longer serve you.

The stories.
The beliefs.
The feels that do not lift you.

The past that drags you backward ten steps every
time you take two forward.

Oh how painful was that way of being for me.

Stepping forward, being seen, only to cry foul and
retreat, retreat, retreat!

I'm going to close with a life-changing thought:

Forgive.

If that caught you off guard and brought up the hairs
on the back of your neck, *good*. There's something for
you here.

Forgiveness releases *guilt, resentment, bitterness,
shame, blame.*

Forgiveness can release *you*.

From old stories
and that is exactly what you want, is it not?

When those old stories are shed, there is room, an
opening, an allowing to craft anew.

And it starts with *forgiving yourself.*

For the lost time.
The false starts.
The sabotage.
The anger.
Frustration.
Shame.
Blame.

If you want to begin today,
creating new delicious stories,
start by forgiving yourself
and *allowing what was to be.*

This right here is the best way forward,
one known intimately by those most happy.

no more rearview you

What if you knew you were exactly where you are meant to be each and every moment?

Allow that thought to sink in and wrap you in comfort, as it is *#truth* . . .

That you could not get this next step wrong.

That there is no wrong step to take
for every step leads you to another,

so long as you are willing to move forward,
releasing the need to slide backward
into the rearview of you.

You are here, reading these words, because you are *ready* for this message.

You are *willing* to hear and capable of stepping up to the plate of you, doing the work to create your most delicious life, are you not?

You are all in.

What would be possible if you allowed your past to stay there?

Not taken out daily, weekly, monthly, yearly
to beat yourself up with,
to poke, blame, or shame another
or yourself with.

When you can let go of the "failures"
and simply focus on today's opportunities . . .

When you can see you are fully supported,
understanding all happens as it is meant to . . .

When you can allow,
instead of tight fisting your way through life . . .

Magic *will* unfold in your now.

You are here. Now.

You can spend it looking backward or you can sink
into this moment and be fully, completely,
JOYfully present.

It may feel weird, *strange*.

It may take some work to remind yourself to step out
of the past and into today, and that's okay . . .

Stop judging, dissing, expecting yourself to get this
work, this concept—anything—*immediately*.

Stop expecting *perfect*, as there is no such thing,
especially when faced with something brand-new,
which this may be.

Just *allow*.

And see what shifts as you stand firm in being
here today,

How would it feel in your body . . .
to let go of the past that no longer serves you . . . ?

The you who forgives yourself for lost time
and sees nothing but opportunities,
endless possibilities to focus on in the *now*.

letting go

Letting go is first about forgiving yourself and then forgiving others . . .

Forgiving yourself for the wrongs, the slights, the stories you keep carrying around that dragged you down to the muddy ground.

If you say you want to fly,
if you say you want to live your most delicious life,
forgiveness is key.

And it starts first with forgiving yourself for *thinking, feeling, believing* you are doing this thing called life *wrong.*

You aren't. You didn't.

The only thing "wrong" is to think you did.

That is nothing more than a story.
Are you ready to let that shit go?

If that's a story you can now acknowledge
as having been alive within you,
you can *choose* to let it go.

Release it.

173

Or you can keep hanging onto it—a most heavy *stone-story* to carry.

I often work with my clients on *forgiveness letters—* not a new concept, certainly not one I made up, but one that works wonders when you purple pen it with *a twist of deliciousness.*

If you want to speed dial this new you into existence . . .

If you're ready to *let go, release,* and *move forward* into a new way of showing up . . .

It's time to forgive you.

Instead of writing a forgiveness letter to another— someone who has wronged you, hurt you, betrayed you, or judged you harshly—

write a forgiveness letter to you.

Yourself.

It's time.

And if you're thinking, *Forgive me for what?* I hear you loud and clear, as this used to be me.

What about all those stories you've chosen to believe that do nothing more than beat you up?

What about those names you call yourself in broad daylight? In the dead of night?

What about those negative thoughts you harbor about *not being enough*?

When you're ready,
forgive yourself for all that's held you back.

Imagine as you do that each thought, story, belief served you.

Sink into gratitude . . .

for that wrong turn you think you made
even though you truly did not.

There is no *right* path,
no *wrong* way,
only this step forward.

Today.

Forgive yourself by writing a letter, and I can guarantee that this work is what will enable any deep-seated turmoil, drama, stress, and so much bottled-up emotion to flow out.

Let it all out. With your words for only you to see.

The point is to feel what's been locked within,
allow what's been festering to erupt, spew out.

Don't judge it, don't push it down,
as this right here is your way to release it . . .

for you.

What would it *feel* like
to be free of all those
woulda, shoulda, coulda thoughts.

Thoughts, beliefs, stories
that are simply a way to bring you
down,
down,
down.

Forgiveness is powerful solo work.

Work best released with fire
or tossed off a cliff—
safely, of course—
when done penning the words.

**I think it's important to reiterate that *nobody*
is to read this.**

Forgiveness work is really an *inner* work
*and the one thing that will propel you forward like
nothing else. . .*

when you do it and let it go.

It's vital this letter of forgiveness or any journal you pen
not become a new altar for your suffering . . .

Not become a new story you share, reread, and spin in.

Don't spoil the power of journaling by relapsing into the old stories when you're down.

Better to give your words to the elements of earth, fire, air, or water.

Set them, and yourself, *free*.

a forgiveness letter

Start today by writing yourself a forgiveness letter
from your heart.

When you do you can soar.

Write it out . . . as described above, making sure you
block out some uninterrupted time.

Give yourself the space,
the grace,
to pen words from your heart.

It may be about *one line you say to yourself on repeat*,
one story you believe that is truly not kind.

It may lead to an outpouring of events or things said
that you feel are past time to release.

Simply allow what comes
to come through you.

To empty onto the page.
No judgement.
No shame.
No blame.

When you do and allow it out,
you will feel *lighter, freer, clearer,*
and more able to create a life

that makes you shiver with delight
as you open your arms wide to possibility.

**When done, give yourself grace and space to
feel all that you feel.**

Forgiveness is an energetic workout of the body, mind,
and soul.

Rest, nourish, allow yourself to heal.

And schedule that moment,
within that same twenty-four-hour day,
to burn or release that which you wrote
so it's gone and done,

no longer a weight for you to feel.

In the daylight.
In your once sleepless night.

twins

I once picked up a set of twins, one by one.

One was blonde and feather-light, full of laughter, sunshine, and rainbows. She giggled and was forever craning her neck. . . *what delights awaited she?*

The second, just minutes older, had rich gold curls and a serious frown.

When I went to lift her, same size and shape as her twin, she seemed to erect a force field around her small body, pulling with *all her might* to the ground.

Where the first laughing girl launched herself upward, propelling her little body, this more silent one seemed to physically retreat, literally edging herself back and away.

As though hiding in plain sight.

I so related to this second child who was oh-so heavy when I finally hefted her into my arms. She rested on my cocked hip, a grubby hand grabbing for my ponytail as she refused to meet my eyes . . .

Looking down, not so much around. But she, contemplative and quiet, was incredibly intent, alert, aware when her eyes finally did meet mine.

Her focus—*deep, personal, wise.*

Not caught up in finding JOY everywhere, anywhere.

Not that there's anything wrong with that fun-loving way of being.

Two girls, raised in the same home yet so very different—*energetically.*

Everything is energy and everything about this *heavier* little one required more care, more awareness as she was the one *who took all to heart.*

Who made it a story right from the start.

She was absorbing the world,
feeling all the emotions,
while her sister ebbed and flowed easily
like the most peaceful, playful tide.

I was this little girl who found life so heavy.
Made myself heavy.

Even when I wanted to launch myself upward and have fun, to giggle and laugh like another, I found myself first *observing, spinning a tale, running all my known-to-me programs*—stories—in the background of me.

For me, I was only light and airy while on my bike racing down a hill—*free falling.*

Or sharing deep, spellbinding tales with my furry forest friends.

Just like that older twin, the one who made herself physically *heavy*, there are some of us who go through life doing the same.

Physically. Emotionally.

Marinating in a *negative* story. A story that no longer benefits, simply because it's known, familiar, comfy in its confining naturalness.

We do it all the time.

I've done it on repeat my entire life . . .

Stayed entrenched in those negative tales,
spinning them,
refusing to fully pull the threads
because if that story truly disappeared,
I might as well too . . .

For shattered, scattered
into a million broke-ass pieces
is what I'd feel.

But now, in my forties,
I see the utter yumminess of going all in
and nixing stories
one by one.

I don't propel myself up without thought,
like that first twin—
laughing with delight.

That's simply not my way,
and perhaps not yours as well.

I used to make myself *wrong* for not being *easy* like she.
For not being more fun, more carefree.

Yet, being the observer, feeling the feelings of all, is me.

Interesting how we tend to hate the very way we are
naturally made, created. Always believing there is a
better way to be . . .

Now I simply own me being me.
No longer judging so harshly,
no longer making it wrong
to be me.

Just as I didn't blame that twin for being who she was,
my new story is learning to no longer blame me
for who I be.

And that means,
the way I root to the ground
isn't good or bad,
isn't meant to be compared
to another's light, carefree approach . . .

But is meant to be accepted,
appreciated,
loved . . .

As a quality that creates the entirety of me.

What if you did the same starting today?
No longer made how you show up *right* or *wrong*.

Just show up as you, stop judging and ask,
Does this way of being serve me, benefit me?

If yes, that's a #win.

This is what creates a deliciously magical life.

It's past time you put down the *struggle* sword
and pick up a new *word* weapon
that you yourself can spin in . . .

One that lifts you up,
even if you naturally sink to the ground.

One that allows you to smile wide,
even if just *internally*
as you know you are not broken . . .

Not meant to be any other way.

When you're ready to do just that, turn the page and
dive into creating your new story, one of divine ease.

As you get to know you.

awareness

We are all living by stories that we didn't agree to.

These stories run our lives.
Until, awareness strikes a pose.
With awareness, comes a shift.

The ability to *shift* or *change* a story.
To *discard* old stories,
to *create* new ones.

Awareness begins with asking great questions, and
the first one to begin asking is . . .

Who am I under all the stories?

Under all you've been *told*
and *bought*
as you were *sold.*

Once you know clearly who you are, then it becomes
easier to answer the next powerful ask.

What do I want?

We've touched on this before and we'll circle back
around in a bit, but for now, focus in on that

Who am I? question without all the stories, and see
what comes your way.

who am I, really?

One of the most powerful writing exercises I recommend to my clients is answering this simple yet so-very-complex question:

Who am I?

Ask yourself that now and notice what you feel in your body.

Who am I?

Resistance.
A tightening of muscles,
a clogging of your throat.

Or curiosity in the form of
a tickle, a thrill, a shiver of excitement.

When you start down this path, it can become fascinating to pay attention to your own inner and external reactions.

This is how you get to *know* yourself.

Consider really tapping into this way of being for yourself as you keep reading these pages, and I promise you, you will get to know yourself so very well you will want to kiss me.

Okay, maybe not *kiss, kiss,*
but I promise you,
when you sink in and answer this question
in deep-detail,
your life will not look the same
thirty, sixty, ninety, one hundred eighty days from now.

It starts with blocking off twenty-two minutes to ask
yourself one question:

Who am I?

Your challenge, your task, write *nonstop* on what
comes to you.

Pen to paper, *go.*
Need more time? *Allow.*
No pausing to edit, no judging what you put down.

Anything goes.

Play in childlike wonder and answer:

Who am I?

Wake up the next day and ask yourself today,
in this moment:

Who do I want to be?

Then spend thirty minutes, nonstop, pen to paper, and
write out this new version of you.

These two questions will allow you to tap into

who you are today and *who you desire to become* by simply shining light on that new version of *you*.

Remember to write *present tense* and *positive* as you answer both of these questions:

Who am I?
Who do I want to be?

This is the start of creating what I call *The Alter Ego You*.

4: Changing the Story

Changing the Story

Flipping the script of a story can be *easy*
or it can be *hard*.

Every coin has two sides.

You can believe
that the side you get is not up to you,

or you can grab that coin mid-flip
and *choose* the outcome,

an outcome
that rocks your world
in a most *delicious* way.

shedding

It's a simple shedding of one story, one layer, one old fuzzy sweater that's got so many holes you can clearly see how it no longer serves.

It's a removal of that item,
that story, that fabric
that no longer keeps you warm
at night.

That once-comfy, known thing
is actually what's snuffing out your light, swallowing you in once-comforting folds.

Sometimes it's literally as simple as the shapeless clothes we wear.

The boxy, tent-like cut that hides who we really are under it all as we walk around in stark sunlight.

The drab colors that allow us to blend in.

The hunched shoulders that enable us to believe we go unseen.

The shyness we label and hide behind.

How would it feel to stand proud and see those curves of yours without hate?

To wear a pop of hot pink or a full array of all the
colors *if it pleases you* . . . ?

To be able to say *I love myself*
and feel a bloom of delight?

To square those shoulders,
tilt your chin up,
allow your lips to form a grin?

Now that's you *being* delicious.

Or it can be as *complex*
as the relationship
that feels like a wet blanket,
suffocating in its toxicity.

*How would it feel to no longer accept being spoken to
in such a negative way?*

By another? By your own voice rumbling in
your head?

To put your foot down and say, "No more!"
drawing a line in your sand?

No one ever again *allowed, enabled, trained*
that it's okay to speak to you in such a way?

To retrain the voice within?

To be able to whisper, "I am enough"
and feel a ripple of divine *truth*?

That right there *is* the work.

A learning to step into a *new version of you* in this moment where the *current you* still exists.

It's playing in the delight of possible new thoughts, new ways of feeling about yourself, about the world, about others.

When this way of showing up—
in the sandbox you play in,
those castles,
once only in your dreamt-up sky
will become the very thing you walk amongst.

And that is the greatest all-natural high.

For me, it was basic and started with one *I am* statement—

I am a writer.

Imagine if you allow that version of you to stop playing hide-and-seek,
to step out into the sunlight.

See how that feels.

Write that *you* down.
Take that *you* for a test drive.

Of course, you can't make yourself six feet if you're really five feet two inches, but you can certainly

embody the energy, the *presence* of a six-foot
Amazon with long legs and even longer hair.

You can walk into a room and feel six feet tall, can
you not?

You can strut, a swing of your hips . . .
if you so desire.

This is where you get to play,
to create the *you* you want to *become*.

When you do, something delicious comes undone.

The ties that bind you,
hold you back,
they start to slip free . . .

As if when you start
being the you of tomorrow *today*,
you become the you

you say you want to be.

flip the script

Imagine if *changing your story* doesn't have to be a struggle.

What would be possible if you flip your script—simply by telling one of your stories from another perspective.

Then flip it again and again and again.

How many perspectives does a story have?

Way more than you think.

There's a tale of three men and an elephant—a fable that's been retold again and again.

Perhaps you've heard it.
If so, sink in with fresh ears.

Three blind men are *considering* an elephant.

> The man who touched the trunk declared, "A snake."

> One touched his leg. "Oh, it's a tree trunk."

> Another touched the tail and said, "No, it's a rope."

They're seeing the parts, not the whole—*story*—of the elephant.

How often do we see *a piece, a section,* or *a point of view* of a story and jump to a conclusion?

Have you ever assumed something, having only one piece of the puzzle?

She doesn't like me. She looked at me funny.

Maybe she simply had something in her eye.

Perhaps a sudden bout of indigestion hit her hard.

You may remind her of the daughter she just argued with.

The teacher never calls on me. He thinks I'm stupid.

Maybe he doesn't see your hand *half*way up.

Perhaps he takes your frown as *leave me alone, having a bad day.*

Maybe he calls on the first person he sees.

Maybe he knows you *get* the material and is giving another time to shine.

That asshole cut me off. Crazy driver out to get me.

Maybe she's running late or got into a fight with her lover.

Perhaps she did not even see you, *Boo!*

Maybe she never even learned how to drive
as good as you.

What if it's not about *you* at all?

How much longer are you willing to carry around the
heavy weight of stories that don't serve you and may
very well be based on *false* info or a lie?

Often it's our very stories that limit us from seeing the
whole picture, *just like that elephant*, if we allow it.

And typically we're not even aware that we're the ones
limiting ourselves.

Ah, responsibility—*again.*

That's what we call a blind spot, and my job as a
writer, a teacher, a coach interested in impacting one,
you, is to pull out my flashlight and shine the light on
that which is not easily or often seen.

In fact, this is what my coach does for me.

Yep, I have a coach—

a great one who has allowed me to step into my own
greatness in numerous ways. Allowing me to see that
stepping from the shadows of life, becoming visible,
*hell, even writing these here words and publishing
them as me doesn't have to be scary . . .*

Which I must say has been as *easy* as it has been a *struggle* . . .

Because of an old story I have that's been on replay within me forever.

Hider is me.
Ghostwriter am I.

This is a story I have spun again and again.
Internally and externally.

Making it oh-so negative.

When, is it really?
Negative?

Or is that right there the story?

What stories do you spin in over and over again?
What interpretations do you make?

When you perfect flipping the script, you get to see all the pretty and not-so-pretty angles. . .

ownership

A mistake that's so common
I see it time and time again,
one that I perfected for decades,
was to own what was wrong, bad . . .
what I so wanted to change.

In owning *my* sickness, in calling it *mine*, I perpetuated
the continual creation of that very thing I didn't want.

"I am sick" keeps the story alive.

"I am anemic" keeps me spinning in low iron,
near death's door again and again.

"I am healing" allows me to flip that script,
shift my flow.

When you change
the story,
tune,
way of speaking,
journaling,
repeating . . .

You shift your way of *being.*
And that's a delicious thing.

"The tongue has the power of life and death."
—Proverbs 18:21

Don't get nervous or excited here as I'm not taking us to church.

Although some Southern Baptist ladies sure know how to get their groove on. *Sing, sisters, sing!*

I quote the Bible here as it sums up your, every single beings, personal power as a creator—*brilliantly.*

Lean in for a moment and feel the difference.

Say to yourself or out loud—
I am (negative) *statement*

Then say the opposite.
I am (positive) *one.*

I am sick. (negative)
I am healing. (positive work in progress)

I am healthy. (*Yes!* Positive who you be!)

The trick is to begin to create your life now, in *present positive*, even when you feel as though you are not.

For how can you heal when all you think, feel, say, repeat, believe is *I am sick*.

You are what you say you are.

Your life is the way you say it is.

Sometimes that right there is a mighty hard pill to swallow.

The way to dash it down with JOY is by telling empowering new tales of what you want—*not what you don't.*

Words are powerful.

Isn't it time you own them, rock them, and use them with intention to support your fabulous self?

status quo

Let's travel back to brunch with the ladies. Remember we spoke of one ordering a salad and the convo that ensued quickly turning to body shaming.

Hell, *life shaming.*

Now imagine ordering a plate of Belgian waffles at that brunch, topped with strawberries and a generous dollop of cream.

You grab the syrup, *unafraid.*

You share with these women at the table,
your friends, that you love your body—
each curve, each nook, and cranny.

You love your body's strength,
ability to heal itself,
ability to feel pleasure and pain,
all of it.

It's not about the waffles or anything you eat.

It's about you,
your attitude,
your *belief* in you.

Imagine telling a group of women, "I love myself."

Congratulations.
You have just changed the story.
Disrupted the status quo.

Some women will *love* this freedom, your energy.
Some will feel *threatened* by it.

And it's none of your business how they feel.

**Freedom comes when you focus instead
on *how you want to feel* in each moment of
every day.**

Yet for many the first thought that may pop up is, *But
that's selfish!*

And I cry foul—*that's just another story*.
One you've been sold.
One you bought.

Yet one you now get to ask, *Do I want to still own?*

What if your *only* concern is to focus on how you feel
in that moment?
In each moment?

That, my friend, when you do, leads to freedom.
To peace.

To so much delicious JOY.

your choice

What story do you want to live?

One of discord, *dis*-ease?

A story centered in, anchored in *self-love*?

I start and end my day the same way—I brush my teeth and say, "I love myself."

Toothpaste sprays everywhere.

It's hysterical, which makes it a great way to start the day.

And a most perfect way to end my day.

Laughter.
A sound of JOY.
Fully expressing myself.

When I first started, I didn't like saying this phrase—
I love myself.

It all but made me cringe.

And no, I did not believe it.

I truly, deeply, honestly didn't love myself.
And that was the *root* of so much suffering for me.

See, I grew up hearing that I wasn't lovable from one who you'd think would sing your praises. But that wasn't my path.

But please, don't cry for me, Argentina.

My path was my path.

To hear I was *too sensitive.*

To be a worrier.

To lack self-confidence.

Because it led me here . . .

To being able to purple pen words
that perhaps will shine a light for you
on what it might look like to change your own tune.

To sing your praises and no longer diss you
and instead craft a most delicious story that
supports you.

one story changed adds up

Start with a small story.
Perhaps something recent,
something that didn't go the way you wanted it to.

A promotion.
A conversation with a loved one.
A decision you made.

Are you replaying this story in your head over and
over again?

If not, pick one that you do replay again,
wishing for another outcome,
another chance at something left unsaid . . .

Wanting to believe that if only you'd done this,
said that,
been more
assertive,
kind,
firm,
loving,
forceful,
strong,
you—

it would have turned out differently.

What stories are you spinning, replaying,
a slow leaking of all your power,
desiring a different outcome?

Wishing, hoping, and even *praying*
are a trap that keeps you stuck
unless you also *move your feet.*

Changing a story is a great way to start moving in a
new, *powerful-is-you* direction.

Whatever your stories are,
it's time to flip the script . . .

Tune into a new station,
play another album,
and sing a new tune.

Once you have the tale you want to shift, ask yourself
a few questions. Jot down your answers in your
own delicious journal, as the act of writing is more
empowering than you know.

Is holding on to this story serving me?

Is holding on to this story holding me back?

If it's serving you, keep playing it on repeat.

But if it's not,
don't you owe it to yourself
to scratch that record
and put on a new track.

What's a new way to spin this tale?

Or is it possible to simply let it go?

Letting go is an important skill to learn and master because truly the only thing you have is this moment.

Reading these words.

Yet how often are you transported back in time, to a tale long done yet replaying in your mind, influencing who you choose to be on this day?

A story from what? Ten, twenty, thirty years long gone . . .

Imagine what could bloom in the garden of you if you were willing to finally let that aged web go.

Write out what your life is
without all the energy
going to the spinning
of that web

and when you're ready to seriously say *adios,*
let me know.

a most careful tongue

Proceed with caution: Take care with your words.

The universe
(or God or whatever word yanks your chain)
is always listening, *without bias,*
watching, *without mercy,*
and giving you *exactly* what you ask for.

With your thoughts, with your words, with your tall
tales spun.

When you take ownership of that which you say,
when you use words intentionally . . .

Never spitballing just to hear yourself talk . . .

You will begin to see the force behind your words,
any words uttered,
and begin to speak with more care.

You become a powerful mother—
cough
creator of your very life.

A powerful unstoppable, unshakable, badass force.

And *that* I want to see.

shifting dialogue

Now if you're asking, *How do I . . .*

> ➤ *change the story?*

> ➤ *stop the cycle?*

> ➤ *create a new story?*

That's great. Those are great asks.

But really, *how is none of your business* as another's way will not be your path.

You simply start—with utter, profound awareness and allow the rest to unfold as it naturally will.

I changed each story by focusing on first stopping *the inner and exterior dialogue.*

And for many, that's uncomfortable because we suddenly realize just how little else there is to talk about—*with some people.*

With yourself.

Commiserating with a friend about *weight* or *bad relationships* or *money woes* feeds the energy of that story, giving it more power in your life.

Restating the story but repeating things like *There's never enough money* or *We can't afford that* keeps that tale alive.

Having negative thoughts taking up space in your head, now that's a powerful way to keep a story alive. And one we've already touched on.

So let's stick with the conversations we engage in with those in our lives.

Next time when chatting with someone, consider staying *positive* and in *present* tense.

See how the *energy* in the conversation, in yourself, and in others *shifts*.

If you're stuck wondering exactly what stories you may be spinning, *no stress.*

Tap into the *shoulda, woulda, coulda* thinking within you, and you will find oodles of tales—very few of which probably serve you.

We start building these types of stories early in life.

➤ *How we should think*

➤ *How we should behave*

➤ *How we should look and act and feel*

Women are nurturers, therefore should be *maternal.*

Women should be *modest.*

Women should *care about their appearance.*

Really look at all the ways you've been told you *should* be.

Girls are sensitive—
oftentimes told, too sensitive.

But in the same breath,
Don't be too strong as that will make you a bitch!

Boys *should be* strong; therefore, boys don't cry.

Guess what?
Everyone cries.

If we weren't meant to, we wouldn't have the ability to.

Those are all just stories. Even the "nurturing" story.

Not every woman is maternal and to make that good or bad, right or wrong, creates the story that leads so often to suffering for so many.

Sometimes, stories pose as facts.

Remember when milk did a body good?

What about when eggs suddenly became bad for you? Too much cholesterol, was it?

What about stories around coconut oil being all the craze—until it wasn't so healthy for some anymore.

Science—it's only *right, correct, accurate* until it's not.

Science is filled with stories, proven hypotheses,
that are based on the *limits of what we know,
what we can imagine* in a moment of time.

Yet science is often seen as fact. Until it's not. Facts
that make up what we *think* and *understand* about
ourselves, our world, our universe.

Stories are everywhere. Even in science.

The Earth was once considered flat.

The sun, the stars, even the moon—
all, at one time,
rotated around the Earth.

I could go on with more of what was once thought to
be fact, not story, but let's simply sum it up this way:

A story, any story, is a shaky place upon which to build a
life—your life—unless it's a story instinctively true to you.

So as everything is a story,
why not begin choosing, keeping, crafting
only those stories that bring you JOY
and lay a solid foundation
at the root of you.

The knowledge, the fact,
that *all is story*—
that's glorious.

Yet as a human being,

unless you are taught to filter out most of the stories,
many end up being detrimental

to your idea of *success,*
your health,
your relationships,
how you see yourself,
your very state of mind.

Be aware of the stories you hear, repeat, believe . . .
they are everywhere.

changing my story-tune

I have a lot of stories around, hiding in plain sight.

From hiding my body
as a child
behind oversized t-shirts

To hiding myself in weight gain
as a teen
as a young, uncertain me.

How ironic,
to become both large
and more invisible—
unseen.

And as you may recall,
my desire to hide began oh-so young
in other ways too.

Hiding my voice,
hiding my words,
my writing,
my very career.

Then hiding my opinions,
my thoughts,
my deepest self.

Forever trying to be what everyone else wanted me to be.

Or who I thought others wanted me to be.

Hiding in plain sight both served me and hindered me.

Two sides of a beautiful story-coin,
no need to make one side right
or wrong.

Hiding allowed me to tap into my JOY,
my imagination,

something no one could touch
nor take away
like a toy.

When all hell seemed to be breaking apart around
me or inside me, I was able to ground, to center in my
world of words.

And that was a beautiful thing.

To freely be me between the lines on a blank page.

Writer's block? Ha!

That never scared,
never stopped me.

No, my worry—would there be enough time?
Would I be able to pour *me* fully onto the page?

To say all that was forever left unsaid,
quietly.

But now, now as you can see, that word-tune has
changed because here I write, freely as me.

Here I am published, visibly as me.

Just Jill.

No need to hide little old me.
No need to step out into a larger-than-life spotlight.

Changing the story about myself,
about going unseen,
about no longer needing
the comforting cloak of hiding in plain sight

that one, for me, took time
took work

to see it was rooted in a story of shame, of self-blame.

To be seen was to be vulnerable.

To be vulnerable was to be weak.

To be weak was to be a victim
and victim was not me.

So, therefore, I have gone most of my life
purposefully unseen.

One story can shape so very much.

**What story has both supported you and kept
you small?**

**What story are you now considering judging as
wrong?**

Press pause on making anything good or bad
and simply observe.

See stories are not a single thread but often a ball of
tangled yarn.

My story of hiding in plain sight was a
multilayered affair.

Both a decadent dessert
where I could fully spice up my life,
stir the ingredients of me oh-so slowly.

And a pair of fuzzy handcuffs
forever locking me, rocking me
back into place.

And both ways of being served me well.

sixty seconds—go

If you had sixty seconds to choose,

What word would most impact you today, now, in
creating your most delicious life?

Don't worry, you can relax.

Notice how you reacted to the time limit.
Or chose to not.

Simply store that physical reaction away for a beat as
that may be something to sink into later.

If you felt a flutter in your belly,
a hitch of your breath . . .

Remember the essay . . . *frigging dishes?*

My hands in that dish soap transporting me
back, back, back
to that island.

That first-night argument
between The Frenchman and I.

For all is stored at a cellular level and there for you
to uncover.

A story . . .

How delicious to excavate later.

In this moment, where you and I sit having a
heart-to-heart, know there is no time
limit here.

In picking a word that will most impact you.

In rooting out stories one by one and letting them go.

No test to take and pass or fail.
No grade at the end of this stanza.

No *good* or *bad* status thrust upon you.

There is simply *an art to being decisive.*

To *making* a choice.
To no longer *wavering* in life.

And this is something anyone can learn
and if you've ever been like me,
may want to.

Hemming and *hawing,*
paralyzed, *unable to act . . .*

So afraid of making the *wrong* decision, you end up
making *none.*

And that becomes your do-nothing pick. Your choice.
Your decision.

If you've ever come unglued,
or felt stuck,

unable to answer . . .

Feelings of *I don't know*
welling into a silent scream within
when pressed for an answer to any question,

to this very ask:

What do I even want?

Then I encourage you to set a twenty-four-hour
clock and dip your entire right foot into the pool of
just decide, just choose as that is when you begin to
become a pro.

Choose your word for this read
—*not even the year*—

just one word to represent you
for the time it takes you to finish this book.

If you can't give it to me now in sixty seconds,
then set an alert for twenty-four hours from this
moment in time

and choose to give your best *known-to-you* answer
then or before.

Period.

No more *hemming* nor *hawing* allowed.

No more allowing life to pass you by, too afraid to make a choice.

If what's got you stuck is not picking a word,
but leaving a job,
ending a relationship,
saying *I do* to something or someone you love . . .

Set that same twenty-four hour clock and simply make a choice when the bell tolls.

Your choice will never be wrong
but simply lead you
to the next lush valley
or steep, glorious climb
of your most delicious life.

The only way *not* to get there, anywhere, is to *make the choice to remain where you are*—stuck, indecisive, paralyzed.

devoted

If your word of the year is *devotion*, for example, what would that mean to you?

To show up in all things *devoted*.

Pretty powerful way of being, no?

Imagine if you were devoted in your relationships. Even—*no, especially*—the relationship you have with *yourself*.

What would change in your life if *devotion* became your new middle name?

Now that's a delicious thought . . .

I am devoted to my self-care.

And you may even be asking, *Well, what does that even mean?*

Good question.

It's worth a look-see.

What would taking care of you
as you would a child,
a favorite pet,
that car you so love to sink into

with its plush leather seats,
look like?

Only *you* can say.

No one can tell you what you need.
No one can say how best to care for you.

One day, I wrote in my journal,

"I am an *extraordinary* partner to my Frenchman."

And, oh boy . . . was that an eye-opener.

To be *extraordinary* is to be "very unusual or
remarkable," and I was hit upside the head with just
how *ordinary* I was choosing to show up with him.

From arguing to not listening—*frigging dishes*—
I was being far from extraordinary.

Having awareness around how I was showing up,
where I was blaming him when really it was also
me, was a real *barn-burning, eye-opener, grow-up
moment.*

And then to actually consider,
*What would it look like to be extraordinary in this
relationship?*

In our work together, in our life together, in our
communication, in all areas.

It took me being *intentional* with my words, with my

actions, with my reactions to begin to work from a place of *extraordinary*.

That is the power of a word.

Just one word.

To *embody* that word you choose,
whether it be *devotion* or *extraordinary*,
literally changes all.

When you choose a word of the year, month, duration of this read and focus on it daily, with intention, everything changes in your life.

dating you

My word for the year is my name: *Jill.*

It sounds simple, right?

Holy Moly, it's not. It's kicking my ass.

I'm having to get to "know thyself" deeply, intimately, *all the nooks and crannies.*

Choosing me,
my name,
as my word of the year
has been like *dating* myself.

A real *get-to-know-me* moment in time.

Definitely a dating phase, a slight tiptoeing around me.
Not yet a relationship nor a honeymoon moment in time.

This has been the year of first, second, and third dates
with me, myself, and I.

Have you ever taken time to literally *date* yourself?

Imagine if you did.

This year I am dating me.
I'm getting to know me.

I'm getting to fully, deeply trust me,
to hone in and hear my voice—*fully* . . .

Not looking externally for *answers*
or validation for my stories.

No longer *case-building* to keep my limitations.

I'm tuning into my own inner voice.

My inner *knowing*, that delicious mini-me. . .
massive-inner-me.

And it's been lovely.
And hard as all hell.

Purple Pen
PRACTICE

what's in a word...?

When you consider your word,
whether for the time it takes you to read this book
or for a year,
sink into how that word makes you *feel*.

Allow all your senses to *engage* and *lean in*.

Your word will *teach you so much about yourself* when
you let go of all expectations and begin to embody it
minute by minute . . .

Not as a race to some imagined finish line
but into the *Journey of You*.

And I for one, can't wait to hear it's impact.

Don't be surprised if your word introduces you to
stories you hold dear.

Stories you now begin *to question, to see as
limitations, to release.*

Imagine what's possible if you simply *give no meaning
to what comes up.*

Accept what fits,
reject that which no longer serves,
and *observe* your ebb and flow.

As when you do, *you grow*.
And that, my friend, is your path to deliciousness.

white baby goat

If you want to see how much power your words have, I'm going to encourage you to enJOY the white baby goat experiment sometime this week.

Tell yourself, *I will see a white baby goat today.*

Random, right? Sink in anyway.

Place your *attention* and your *focus* on a white baby goat. Look at a picture of one online if it helps. Get a dose of cuteness and smile because when your senses, your happy is engaged, you are more powerful than you even know.

Here's what I know. You *are* going to see a white baby goat.

It might be a long-haired white baby goat or a short-haired one.

It might be a video of one hopping about or a photo of someone in a yoga pose with a baby goat invading their *downward* dog.

Goat yoga. *For real!*

That white baby goat will be there . . .

Somewhere, crossing your path.
Soon.

Maybe you'll see it on the road,
or on a billboard,
or on television,
or in a meme,
but it will be there.

In a children's book
you read to your own little one tonight,
a goat previously not even noticed.

In a card you receive from a friend.

Simply pay attention and allow that white baby goat
to be.

And this is key and the point—
*what you focus on in thought
or with the words you speak,*
exists.

Simply because you give it power,
energy.

And you know from these pages and my repetitive
voice, *everything is energy.*

So how does this experience of seeing a white baby
goat help you?

It's positive proof that *what you think about shows up
in your life* in one form or another.

Not by your time of

Right now, damn it!
complete with an indelicate foot stomp.

But in the best time,
the moment that will perfectly serve you.

Whatever moment that happens to be.

Give it a go. First with the white baby goat, then with
something else.

A free meal.
A held-open door.
A cup of paid-for-*not-by-you* coffee.

A hundred dollars or more—
leave room for possibility—
unexpectedly landing on your doorstep,
in your bank account, mailbox, paycheck,
or a random unexpected gift.

There are endless possibilities.

You are already a pro at this way of being.
You simply don't recognize your own skill set.

And if you're like so many, you brush it off as
coincidence.

Giving not a second thought,
not a dash of gratitude
to the universe, God
for showing up to *support* you . . .

To give you *exactly* what you ask for with your thoughts, your words.

So why not focus on finding money today instead of bemoaning the lack thereof. . .?

When you do,
focus in receiving
(as though it is done) not from a place of lack,
you will

Find. . .

A penny, a dime, a Euro, or Indian rupee on the street.
Pick that shit up.

Do not disregard it as meaningless,
as *not enough.*

Who are you to say *what will follow* when you *show some respect* for what came your way?

There is a reason we have sayings like
"See a penny, pick it up; all day long, you'll have good luck."

It's not luck, *it's law.*
But that doesn't flow so well, *now does it?*

Simply pick up that penny or note
and give *a smile of thanks,*
keeping your thoughts in gratitude, in *abundance.*

Not dissing the lack of *enoughness*,
as that right there stops the natural flow.

See what else befalls you,
comes your way,
when you sink into receiving
with graciousness,
with gratitude.

Ah, the power of *receiving*—
it opens a door to much.

Check out the resources section
if you need some goat-spiration.

twenty-twenty sight

There came a moment where I saw my stories for
what they were.

Stories of struggle
long come and gone.

Stories I repeated to myself, to others
that did nothing more than *press me down.*

Stories I wrote about from a space of healed,
intentionally sharing
so another could mend
on some big or small level.

And others I kept alive
to suffer through
again and again . . .

Not realizing to do so
was never a punishment
for the one who hurt me
but a trap, a cage

I willingly locked myself in.

**There were even a few stories I planned to
*carry to my grave.***

A warped thought of maybe

if the one to blame
could but see me suffer a lifetime,
they would finally admit to their wrongs.

Finally apologize.
Finally *free me* from the *bondage* of being me.

I will admit there were one or two tales I quickly,
graciously *released with love.*

How I knew to do so, that tidbit was not for me to
comprehend *then.*

But now, *hot damn*, now I know *that path of letting go*
is everything.

To be able to receive such clarity,
to see that *it's the stories you spin in . . .*

That right there is what propels you to great heights
or drags your ass back down again and again.

Your very own personalized *Groundhog Day.*

What you are creating
day after day
with the words you say . . .

The stories you *choose* to swim in,
stories you can change in the blink of an eye . . .

That crystal-clear awareness means you can drop a
story that feels like a heavy weight and replace it with
one that feels ultralight as soon as right now.

When you're ready to feel
weightless . . .
free.

Try it on and see.

5: Telling a New-to-You Story

Telling a New-to-You Story

You can stew
in the newfound
or repeated-sounding—
Everything is a story.

Or you can lean in
with curiosity,
with delicious delight . . .

And consider
all that you can *now* create . . .

That's just out of sight.

It's time to open the floodgates to a most delicious you.

throwing down

Picture me like J-Lo
ripping off her gold hoops right now.

I'm about to throw down on this topic for a minute.
As it's so very important to catch.

Learning to live new stories,
to live with JOY,
to live your most delicious life
is just like learning to walk.

We don't all do it the same way.
We don't figure it out in one day.

We didn't all start walking
at the exact same age
of the same day
on a set hour.

Each one of us learns to walk when *called* to do so.
Some earlier than others.

That doesn't make them *right*.
Or those who enJOY the crawl *wrong*.

Simply different.

Imagine *celebrating* your differences *again*
as you once did as a child.

No longer desiring to
fit in.

Conform,
blend in,
be one with the crowd.

I get it.

The bubble of frustration,
the flush inching up your neck
as you *mentally demand* all the fucking steps.

Imagine me stomping my size-seven flip-flops for
effect.

As that was once me, all up in my head,
wanting the gold-lined pathway *now*.

Thinking, believing
I could get there
if I simply had the manual,
a staircase to self-discovery
laid out before me.

I could follow steps, *damn it all.*
I could climb those stairs *faster than anybody;*
I would be first to *ring that bell.*

But a bell to what?

Where was I in such a rush to go?
What if there is no *there*?

Only here.
Now.

When I discovered this,
it stopped my forward race down *Transformation Trail.*

There is no bell.
There is no end.
There is no prize
to take
for first place.

The only destination in life is death.
Everything else is the journey.

So here and now,
what's possible
if you chose the type of journey
you desire to have along the way?

You get to choose. *Delicious* or bitter-*sharp*.

That's not to say there won't be *highs* and *lows* when
you create your most delicious life. To think that way is
a sin . . .

Kidding. But really, *sink in.*

Anyone who tries to sell you *the perfect life* is full of it,
for there is no such thing. There is life.

Some people enJOY a more *flatline* state of mind,
but if you want a truly *delish* ride,
it comes with ups and downs,

bumpy dirt byways,
and smooth-as-silk highways.

Much like nature,
there is a natural *ebb* and *flow*.

It's not *right*.
It's not *wrong*.
It simply *is*.

Like the tides.
The seasons.

To stop fighting them,
wishing them different than they are . . .

That takes grace.

Because without *hot* you cannot know *cold*.
Without *sorrow* you cannot truly know JOY.

I know this firsthand, and perhaps, so do you.

I share steps and pieces of my journey, as it's how we
learn, but your path will look very different.

And that's delicious . . .
if you choose to see it that way.

the stage

Let's set this stage, one as old as time.

Stories can be full of drama, intrigue, pain, shame.
Stories can be full of love and JOY, curiosity and flow.

This is your moment to decide the new story you want
to tell.

Yep, only one for now.

To bite off more than you can chew leads to a story
of *overwhelm* or *procrastination* or *repeated self-
sabotage*, to name but a few.

My coach likes to say, "Let it be easy."

And here's the golden nugget.
For me, when I do *let it be easy*, it is.

Easy.

You could ask, *Why is that?*—but we just finished
talking about the rabbit-hole spin that word—*why*—
leads to.

Instead of *analyzing, contemplating, staying forever-
in-your-head* like I once did, what if you simply saw
that line right there—*let it be easy*—for what it is?

A story. *Your* new story starting today.
Let it be easy. And so it *is*.

Just as the opposite is also true when you say it is.

And this used to be my operating default.
Let it be hard. *Fool.*

This was how I spoke to myself, internally on repeat.
Berating myself time and time again.

And that right there
was one of the first stories
I chose to flip
just like turning on a light switch.

Let it be easy, this thing called change.

And so it was.
I kid you not, as *easy* as that.

[insert rather loud finger snap!]

That is the power of story.

You hold so much more power than you even know.
The power to say this new story—*let it be easy*—and
allow it to be true.

Now it's up to you to give it a go.

Are you willing to *surrender*
and begin to tell yourself starting today
a new story of *ease* and *flow*?

When you do, so much of the self-imposed pain will go.

memo

I don't know when adults get the memo—
Life is supposed to be serious.

But I'm calling it what it is—*a fucking lie.*

That we're supposed to stop
dancing in the rain, no longer twirl with arms out,
face to the sun . . .

To stop enJOYing each and every moment
like it could be our very last one.

I didn't keep that memo.

I chose to toss it to the wayside,
order my purple rain boots,
and stomp my little heart out.

Rain or shine.

adulting

What if being an adult doesn't entail being so serious?

I'm here to say
stepping in that JOYless direction of adulting
is nothing but regret.

Believing that as *truth* is buying into a lie.

A story *sold* to you,
to so many,
all the damn time.

Like hot and cold can exist in the same space,
JOY and adulting can too.

Don't believe me?

Press pause on being the grown-up within the next
twenty-four hours and do something fun.

Miss coloring outside the lines? Pick up those crayons.

Thought about dancing again and wanted to take it
back up? Do it. Start with a sixty-second dance party
around your kitchen.

And give this a thought—

How often do you put off fun for another day?

the line

Consider this life-changing idea, two-lines I now live by
one I now live every single day by.

**100 percent possible. 100 percent of the
time.**

When you live in JOY, those two lines may just
become your everything too.

Do the writing,
or whatever is your thing,
as long as it makes you happy,
as long as it is part of your JOY.

And sets your heart to sing,
your soul on fire.

Don't do what I do because I say it.
I'm no guru.

Please do not *fangirl* me.
That once *freaked* me the *hell* out.

Then I recognized it as a story,
one that served me,
kept me small, less than,
protected me

until it was no longer needed.

That making an impact in the life of another was more important than my own discomfort.

My own fears.

Letting go of what I thought it meant to be an adult and simply show up—daily, as JOYful, carefree, fun-loving me.

Do what works
for *you*.

rapid reflection

I will say this . . .

Those who *reflect* with pen and paper,
in my humble experience and opinion,
create their most delicious life
with *rapid* speed . . .

With engaged intent
and so much more JOY
than those who do not.

Finding your voice
between the lines
of pages
meant only for you . . .

Now that's a powerful thing.

Even if it's 25 words one day,
250 words the next

Perfect, I say.

Writing is a way to get to *know* you.

Your stories.
Your wins.
Your path.

To begin to *hear* your own voice.

Now for the wannabe writer in you,
do set a word count to hit
each and every day for a set number of days.

No shame, no blame, if you miss it.
Simply *start* again.

Any other way of being is a downward sin.
A spin.

Just *begin*
again.

From physical writing,
to typing,
to audio journaling,
there are numerous ways to write your own heart
out—
be it purple ink like mine *or not.*

Take a *pause.* Find your *best path.*

Commit, with JOYful devotion, and see what unfolds.

I'm gonna bet that
if you journal out
just 100 words a day,
five days a week,
that's 26,000 words in one year.

When you do this,
no fear,

no holding back,
no shame,
blame,
no bitch fest either . . .

Just your words
uncensored on the page . . .

At the end of one year
and 26,000 words written,
you will for sure
know thyself
and thy measure
so much flipping better.

ritual

Imagine, for a beat,
if you made writing
part of a daily ritual
as automatic
as brushing your teeth.

Just make sure the ritual is not another thing that
holds you hostage or keeps you from succeeding
when life shifts on you, as life tends to do.

Even when living a most delicious life, you are never
immune to the high and low tides.

I get the power of ritual.
It's a beautiful thing.
To light a candle,
pour a mug of tea.

Heck, I have a ritual of three . . .
Coffee, tea, and me—

Okay, water
is the third when I write.

When I do anything with words,
three beverages serenade me.

And that's simple to duplicate *worldwide*.

When rituals become another excuse, that's when you know you've crossed the line.

Excuses are your worst enemy.

They are stories created and used
to hold you down,
pull you back,
and allow time to pass
you by
again and again
while nothing changes.

Just your energetic state
plummeting
down,
down,
down.

The important part of the ritual isn't which teacup you use, which chair you sit in, or the direction you face at the most perfect angle.

The ritual is the humming of energy . . .
The automatic switch that alerts you,
Write, Writer, write.

If writing isn't your thang—
good.

You are engaging in *a know-thyself* way of being.
Congratulations.

So what *does* sound like fun to you if not writing?

The thing you could create a ritual around that serves you . . . ?

What is the thing that you want to do like you want to take your next breath?

That way of being that fills you with JOY?

Journal *that* out.

Because if you want to create your most delicious life,
it's not just about *bringing your sexy back*,
it's about getting your JOY on too.

Purple Pen
PRACTICE

find your word-voice

If you are willing to do a word throw down
and find your word-voice, then I challenge you to
step up today.

Imagine if you said *yes* to five days a week, eleven
minutes a day, to *journal it out, baby.*

You might be thinking, *Look, Jill, now you're talking
forty-four minutes a day between this and the last
Purple Pen Practice. I don't have that kind of time!*

And yep, you're right.

First, those mental math skills rock.

Second, I hear you. Forty-four minutes of your day is a
big ask.

But to say you don't have it is a lie.
The truth lies in *where are your priorities, my friend?*

All I can say is *You're worth the time!*

When you know this, own this, you *will* make the time
to do this work.

When you want to fully step into your dream of
creating a life,

a life you are delighted to wake up to each day . . .

You *will* feel that truth when I say
it takes action,
balanced with those *new-to-you* delicious thoughts,
to make it bloom into existence.

These steps, they are the path you wanted
desperately, no?

So now it's time to own that which you say you want
and find your word-voice.

When you *know yourself better than you know
anything else in life*, you become *unstoppable,
unshakable, unwilling* to settle for anything but . . .

Your most delicious life.

If you're up for this committed finding your voice
challenge to better you, let me know.

Don't make this hard. Allow it to be easy and allow
yourself to have fun . . .

If you're not having fun, you might just be doing this
thing called life in an un-delicious way.

It's time to stop that and spice it up.

Start with finding *your* voice today.
Your way.

When you do, I know something profound will shift in you too.

It did for me; it did for hundreds, thousands of others.

Allow this magic to exist for you . . .

Because I'm telling you, if you want to create your most delicious life,
the only step you need to take
is to *find your voice*,
and it starts with finding your words—
day after day after day.

Words that *serve you*,
uplift you,
release you,
engage you,
free you.

So that you can finally be the you you are here to be.

And this, *writing your purple heart out*, is a surefire way.

But again, this is my path and the path I take my clients on, each one choosing their own word count, their own set number of days.

And finding their own unique *wins* from this experience.

And each and every one of them finds numerous ways to celebrate.

Shifts in how they perceive everything.
Shifts in how they feel.

Wins both big and small
are literally guaranteed
when you do one thing . . .

Simply show up.

Half the battle is won when you do.

And that's delicious.

getting high

If you are capable of spinning negative stories that spiral *down, down, down* like a mad trip inside a rabbit hole, you are also capable of spinning *positive stories.*

The delicious thing about positive stories is the upward spin, taking you *higher and higher and higher*—because everything is energy.

A positive story attracts more positivity. It's really rather simple but we overcomplicate most things, a fatal flaw or human condition.

Luckily there is a cure. *Be positive.* Literally.

And yes, it might feel *strange* and *fake* and *awkward,*

Like that first pair of high heels you slipped on inside mom's closet and the wobbly walk that followed.

You didn't kick off those too-big pumps and cry "never again," *did you?*

Or that time you swore you saw a hair on your chinny-chin-chin and started the *man*-shave only to cut yourself.

You didn't stop at the sight of blood, *did you?*

Heck no! You do and do again—until you are catwalk ready or have perfected the five o'clock shadow.

You entered a wave of excitement,
you did the thing,
it turned out okay . . .

You may have
twisted your ankle,
fallen flat,
or left a dollop of blood,
but you did it again and again and again . . .

That's key—*rinse and repeat.*

Until it becomes so common,
so routine you never even have to think about it.

One foot in front of the other . . .
Heeey, supermodel babe!

One scrape, two scrapes up the neck . . .
Close and tight, just the way you like.

Be open to possibility, *even when it feels false.*
Especially when it feels uncomfortable.

You've done it before.
You can do it again.

When you do, you receive an *a la natural* high.

paint by word

When you think, *the universe listens.*

When you speak, *the universe hears.*

When you ask, *the universe responds.*

This is law.

Don't like the word *universe*? Sub in whatever resonates with you, for words are only words, yet the energy, your energy, behind those words *does matter.*

Your words are your paint-by-numbers guide to creating all you desire in this life. See, you are more powerful than you can even begin to fathom.

Heck, just one cell in our fabulous body has enough energy and know-how to power an entire aircraft carrier.

"I have a need . . . a need . . . for speed."

If you've yet to see *Top Gun*, please do, for me. There's a sequel coming out more than two decades after the original even as I write these words.

But the point is not flying fast planes but that one of your cells is capable, has the ability to, the energy to power the entire ship those jets land on.

And when I say *power that aircraft carrier*, I'm not talking about just steering the boat but *all the systems* on said vessel.

One of your trillions of cells can power the engines, the navigation, the communication coms, the many dozens of planes that take off and land, while also supporting a crew of more than 1,000 souls and seeing to all *their* needs.

Can you even fathom that for a moment?

One cell.
Just one.

Of your—*too numerous to count*—delicious cells could run that, all of that.

What power?!

And yet, what are your cells, all of your cells, doing in a regular, average-Joe day?

Besides naturally and effortlessly running *all the systems* of your body?

Sitting *stagnant*.
Worrying. Wondering. Wishing.
Debating. Do-do-doing all the
perhaps not-so-important things.

Praying.

Leaking, leaking, leaking
all the power you have in just one cell.

The infinite ability
to run such a magnificent,
complex structure as an aircraft carrier.

If you but channeled the power, the energy, the
intention of but one cell.

If you perfected, *mastered* using your will . . .
Even if it took a lifetime
of practicing the art . . .

Never fully obtained,
imagine what would be gained.

And yet, if you are like so many, you are *unaware* of
just how much of your own abilities, power, essence
circles the drain before you even fully start your day.

**Imagine if you stopped leaking your personal
power and started to harness all the energy
you are naturally granted in this amazing life.**

Saying *no more* to spinning negative stories . . .

To people-pleasing, caring what others think,
hating yourself, shaming your body,
focusing on another's drama instead of your own
delicious journey.

If one of your beautiful cells
can run such an
intricate vessel parked in the middle of the sea
where so many systems are being used
simultaneously . . .

Then what's possible for you,
in your day-to-day life,
harnessing the power
of even half your fabulous cellular energy?

You, my friend, would be a force *unstoppable*.
You would be *focused forward*.

You would be a *master* storyteller of tales that support
you in *all systems go*.

You would *focus* on your delicious path.

No distractions.
No more drama.

new story, new identity

Who will I be without *this story* or *that tale* may be
unconsciously playing in the background of you

And let me simply say, you will be *free*,
open to receiving something new, more, better.

What if the unknown is where you find your JOY, your
peace and create your most delicious life?

To believe the unknown is bad, scary, not where you
want to go is nothing but a story.

The scenarios that keep you up late at night . . .

The worry, the stress,
the anxious spin of thoughts . . .

Imagine if your mind was a Ferris wheel,
no longer a roller coaster
whipping and spinning at a dizzying pace.

Now a slow, steady build,
a heady drop,
round and round you go . . .

Until *you* flip the switch and *shut it down.*

For the night,
for the day,
forever.

No more reacting, over or under, with hands flying high,
your scream caught on the night air as you plunge
down,
down,
down
again and again.

No more endless loop,
"It's a Small World After All"
playing nonstop in your head,
so unnaturally, repetitively sweet
your ears literally want to bleed.

Gawd!

When you flip the switch,
allow the lights of overthinking to dim. . .

You get to be curious
about the silence
that suddenly rings loud as a church bell.

Imagine if you walked into the unknown
with a skip in your step,
like a child without a clue
that hurt feels can get to you.

Without a certainty that something bad awaits you
for it doesn't have to.

Imagine if you considered the unknown
your personal magical playground
where you get to create your most delicious life.

Imagine putting a new spin
on your night,
your day,
and considering with a sense of discovery,
a sense of confidence,
wonder and delight
that amazing opportunities are your new norm.

Will there be discomfort? *Probably.*

There is an ache that comes with growth.
Like building muscle in the gym.

We say things like "no pain, no gain" for a reason.

Yet it doesn't have to be painful to let go of a story, to
create a new one.

There is a subtle, important difference.
Painful is a choice.

Painful is a choice
to create, to spin
a new story that goes something like . . .

Poor me.

Might sound harsh, but seriously, consider that the
next time you go to complain,
to retell a tale
that does not serve you—

one you give voice to anyway.

Instead, make a new choice to stand in *gratitude*.

From this place, gratitude,
mixed with a dash of possibility,
all will change.

Sink in and rejoice in the *discomfort of your growth.*

saved

Lift your feet and start *walking*.

Start *telling* that new story.

Do the work *from the you* in that new story.
That part is important.

You can't just *wish* and *pray* for a happy ending.
That's the old way.

A way made popular during the time of *The Secret.*

A great book, movie, interview series but also *a
limiting message* of sit on your sofa, see it, believe it,
and it will come. *Om . . .*

Ah, no.

You create it.
You bring all to life,
manifesting it
through your words and deeds.

You may or may not know the story of a man standing
on his two-story roof in the middle of a great storm.

He prays for God to save him as the murky water laps
at the gutters of his beautiful home, now completely
submerged.

A neighbor in a rowboat appears, telling him to climb on in.

"Thanks, I'm good!" He waves the Good Samaritan away.

A kayak comes by with a passenger and a very wet dog. "I'll send the rescue team," the lady shouts into the pelting rain.

"Thanks, I'm good! God will save me."

She shakes her head and paddles away.

A police boat comes roaring up with two officers who toss him a rope, but he refuses.

"Thanks, I'm good. God's on his way."

They issue a warning. "We won't be coming back. It's your choice now to stay."

He gives a thumbs-up and they motor away, unfazed by human nature after all their collective years on the force.

A helicopter descends and a ladder unfolds just feet away from where he perches on the very peak of his once-dry home.

Waves are now thrashing his ankles as the chopper swings wildly in a gust of wind, struggling to stabilize so he can climb aboard.

But he waves them off, *knowing* he will be saved.

His yellow rain slicker glowing in the moving spotlight, he huddles, braced against the elements as the water now licks at his calves.

A single remaining flip-flop, offering little protection, graces one foot.

Hair plastered to his head, his cap taken by a gust, he shivers, watching the helicopter lift out of sight.

"God is going to save me."

When he arrives at the pearly gates, completely dry, and sees God, it hits him that he's really and truly dead. He falls to his knees and cries out.

"God, I prayed to you, and you didn't save me. *Why?*"

To this God simply says,

"I sent you a rowboat,
an aware kayaker,
a police rescue boat, complete with a rope.

You refused all.

"And still you prayed,
believing with such faith.

"So I sent you a helicopter with a ladder, and again you refused.
And still you prayed as my waters continued to rise.

"You, my son, wanted salvation *your* way. You ignored anything that didn't look as you imagined it should.

"So what did you want?
Me on the back of a magical flying unicorn?"

Consider that for a moment after you snort-laugh and come to terms with the point of this tale.

While that last line is *my take* on this fable known far and wide, press pause a second and see if the message applies to you.

We walk around looking for magical flying unicorns, but often the real answer is to grab the rope and hop in the boat.

Or to swim out of harm's way *ourselves*.

To stop expecting answers to show up as we *imagine* they should look.

To stop expecting life to *look* a certain way.

When you pray, move your feet.

At least that's what I say.

allow

What if life isn't about looking a part?

Imagine for a moment that all of this,
each and every day,
is actually, simply, only
about *being* your true self.

That being you, now, in this moment,
perfectly imperfect,
is enough.

Look at what stories you're telling yourself right now.

That's not me.
Holy shit, that's me to a T.

Just sit with this knowledge, all these stories, for just a bit.

As there isn't one story or two to unravel here.

There are reams and reams,
penned and *believed* daily
over a lifetime.

As my very own mentor shared with me, our stories
actually *create* that which we *believe.*

And what we believe *we tend to hold on to like a*
lifeline even if it's the very thing tugging us under . . .
time after time after time.

Consider just one story or belief you hold on to at all costs.

Big or small matters not, there is no grade given at the end of this, no *right* or *wrong*.

This is the work of you.
The Journey of You,
the path leading to your JOY.

And that's magical when you *allow it to be,*
diving into one story at a time and asking,

Do I believe this?
Need this?
Or is it time to let it go?

Or it can feel like overwhelming defeat.

So many stories to unravel.
Too much time lost believing in nonsense.
Ah, victimhood here we go . . .

This is key: *Simply let go.*

Stop the judgement, *blame-shame game*
as that is just a new story to spin in.

How do you *choose* to see your stories and your part in

receiving,
believing,
owning,
retelling them—?

That will determine much.

I don't know about you, but I'd pick *magical* and smile wide.

I'd choose to see the unraveling of what was,
all the stories that no longer serve this new me,
to be a JOYful *and* sometimes bumpy ride.

Not a midnight,
wild ride of blindfolded scary.

Not a drama- filled-ness that leaves one breathless,
struggling to keep up . . .

Crying out in terror and horror, "Why me?!"

Instead imagine being delighted by what's possible
when just one small tale spun
begins to unravel,
comes undone.

Because that way of being is *already* sinking into what
it takes to create and live a most delicious life.

It may feel pretty cringeworthy or like a fifty-pound
weight's been lifted from your shoulders.

Just sink in with no judgement, *pretty please,*
and feel the release
as you perfect the art of *letting go*

with more and more ease.

To judge you harshly is to dislike, to negate.
It's time to end that cycle.

And that right there can be a most difficult feat.

Until you decide to love you
more than hate.

Don't worry, fret, feel out of sorts if this doesn't come easily, naturally . . . *yet.*

All I can say is sink in and allow.

Just the act of sitting with yourself, alone, quietly might feel hard.

And that's okay.

But, guess what?
I get it. I've been there, done that.

Sitting still, wanting desperately to scream
as all the chatter *within* blasts endlessly.

I've been there, thinking, *This is hard; does it even matter? How will being still, fucking silent even help me get to know me, love me?*

And I realized that *this is hard* feeling that threatened to consume me, made me want to quit just moments in . . .

That too was nothing more than a *story*!

A story that kept me knotted, tense,
forever on the verge
of going over someone else's edge.

If you truly want to dive into your most delicious life, the first step is to see that *everything is a story.*

Are you there yet?

Now fully aware
of one or two stories that rule you,
have ruled you?

The tangled web of so many,
the infinite stories

running,
ruling,
controlling,
dictating
your unhappy—
or happy
life.

Every story starts with *the words you choose to use.*

Those words build and create the stories,
all so beautifully or disturbingly intertwined.

You get to decide.

All the pieces of you are deliciously laid out,
and these pages,
your treasure map,
your connecting of all
so you can begin to see . . .

What works for you.

And what no longer serves you.

Purple Pen
PRACTICE

tell yourself a new story

Now is your time to craft a new story.

I'd imagine at this point and time in your delicious read you have uncovered at least one story that does not serve you to keep replaying on endless repeat.

Now is your moment to let it go. As simple or as hard as that.

And when you choose to let it go, you get to replace it with a delicious new tale that lifts you up, one that makes you feel divine in your skin.

Consider this as a practice.

Stare in the mirror for five minutes and notice what unflattering story rears its nasty little head.

Do you first notice those wrinkle lines?

Think *Good Lord, is that a zit?*

Those bags have taken up permanent residence under my eyes!

Or do you see your inner beauty shining through?

Consider the story you trip on each time you look at your own beautiful-to-me face—

as that which trips you up,
plummets you
down,
down,
down . . .

Isn't it time to hold your head high,
to look at yourself with fresh eyes,
to love yourself endlessly?

**What story can you tell yourself that will start
you down this path today?**

Look at my eyes; they're actually rather shapely.
I like the dent in my chin.
I love my hair.
I see that *I am worthy* . . .
I know now that *I am enough.*

Look into your eyes, unflinching for a minute, two, ten
and begin to tell yourself your new story.

Allow what you feel to bubble up and spill out if that's
what happens.

Keep that one story in your mind, in your head . . .

Pushing out the old if and when it tries to sneak back in.

Write down your new story—one line or many on a
page of your journal—and say it out loud three times.

Here's mine.

I am enough.
I love my freckles.
I love myself!

It's *your* line, *your* new story and practice of letting
go of the old tale that does not serve you another
moment.

Now if looking yourself in the eye
feels too intimidating,
choose to start
pen to paper
and craft that tale of you.

Return to your reflection tomorrow and give it a go
with that new story of you in mind.

It's past time to stop hiding from yourself, is it not?
Focus now on a new story, one that supports, lifts you
up, makes all possible.

A new tale that supports

you loving you,
you being the badass you truly are,
you achieving what you desire,
you being the you nagging to be set free,
you being enough

eye-to-eye

Who do you see when you look at you?

Do you even pay attention, or do you choose to focus on only what you believe to be wrong or lacking?

Imagine if you flip the script, toss the coin high, and choose a new side.

This is the start of the *Journey of You.*
A path into *finding, recognizing, owning* your JOY.

What is possible if you choose today to create a story around being enough, perfectly imperfect—you . . . ?

Around understanding you got this, *boo.*

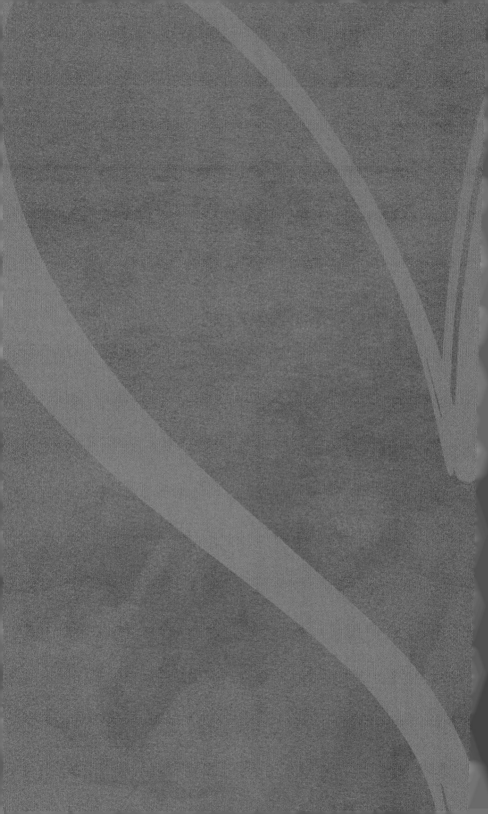

6: Living Your Delicious Life

Living Your Delicious Life

What is delicious to one
may not even tempt another.

If it's in your heart,
that's all that matters.

Follow your own *unique* path
and you will rise up
to a delish life—

one that makes you
giggle and gasp.

a new tale, sung

Letting go of old stories is the opportunity for new
stories to bloom and take root within you.

Stories can be the quicksand that you stay stuck in,
finding it difficult to move forward,
forever pushing on the pull door of life . . .

As you trudge forward,
the weight of the past
all but dragging you back
by your most powerful force,
your very own thoughts.

Or your stories can be grains of sand
that shift through your fingers and drift away.

Released to be forgotten,
forgiven,
blessed as they blow past you—
this way and that way.
Gone in a flash.

And you get to—
choose to—
focus on a new day.

This day.

Let all your stories drift through the cracks of your fingers, weightless.

Allow them to easily float away on a tropical breeze, fading gently, sweetly into that dip in the horizon, where the blue-green sea meets the clear, vivid sky as far as the eye can see . . .

Then puff, *gone*.

That right there is the recipe for peace with a twist of lime—*if you please.*

my start

As I stretch and curl my toes,

typically the sun not yet kissing the seaswept
horizon sky . . .

I give thanks . . .

For my indrawn breath,
deep gratitude.

For my arms and legs and all outside of me,
so much love.

And in my mind,
I say words with intention
to start my day *empowered, blessed, fulfilled.*

Today *is* a delicious day,
a day I get to love myself *completely*.

Today *is* an opportunity,
a day to make this world a better place.

Today I set my attention on feeling JOY,
grace, love, and to make room for a dash of pure play.

Each day those last words shift
but JOY forever remains
as that to me is *my everything*,
my default setting.

The one who's ready for these words and this message—

If you, you may just feel it on an energetic,
spine-tingling level.

Do you? . . .
Feel it?

That delicious nudge to lean in,
to co-create
each day
from this energetic state.

Because you are a co-creator of your life.
And what a magical way to wake up and begin again.

Each and every day.

**What would be possible from that headspace,
that heart-space?**

solar plex-ing

Are you living true *to you?*

If you notice, within these pages, I often mention "pressing pause" or taking a beat.

The time and space to self-reflect is key.

So I'd ask you now to reflect.

Are you living true-blue to you?

Feel that Q deep in your solar plexus.

What's happening in your body as you read that question?

As those butterflies,
that clenching of your gut,
those tightening of muscles,
that tick in the corner of your eye . . .

do not lie.

Have you been living to please another?
To please everyone else . . .
and ended up pleasing none, as I have done . . ?

In the past.

Allow what you feel to be present, and if it calls to you, take a beat to write in your delicious journal whatever it is welling up in you.

open book

If you're anything like most of those I write for, teach, consult, or coach . . .

You too have unearthed a few tales—
that were previously unbeknownst to you—
running in your background
just by reading these pages.

Programs or stories you weren't aware of on a conscious level perhaps but now have a nagging awareness of what may have you thinking—

Oh, shit, I really believe that and that runs my life.

A sudden awareness of the possibility that *many of the decisions you've made are based on that thing that person over there once said.*

And that is the danger of going *outside* yourself for an answer to the deepest and even simplest of questions.

If you ask three different people for advice in one day, you will get three different answers. *Guaranteed.*

If you ask three different people what you should do about your relationship, the job you hate, or how to handle a conversation with so-and-so, you will get three different perspectives. *Always.*

And here's the rub.

You're rarely sharing as a fully open book.

We share pages, paragraphs,
pieces of the story . . .

Think back to that fable of the three men and an
elephant—*a snake, a rope, a tree trunk.*

The danger lies when we share, as we tell the tale in
pieces, rarely as a whole. Often innocently slanted a
certain way.

Prone to provide,
to feed that need within
for validation,
to be seen as right . . .

Then listen intently to another for the path we should
now take and wonder why it leads to more heartache.

This was *so* very much me.

Basing my choices
on the interpretations others received
from the small bits I chose to share,
conveniently leaving out those facts
that didn't serve me looking my best,
you see.

And the feedback—
so freaking confusing.

One answer,
two answers,
three answers.

Like counting sheep . . .

left more clueless which path I should take
as I refused to first tap into myself.

Do I work with that person?

Hire that girl, this guy?

Do I move?

Go out with he?

What do you think I should do, boo?

When you aren't first honest and clear with yourself,
willing to look under the hood
of all those stories you may just hold so dear . . .

Unwilling to share
that which might make you look a fool . . .

Unable to go within,
get silent and feel
what it might feel like to know you . . .

Your own inner knowing.

Now that's a recipe for constant disaster
as peace comes when you first begin to listen to you.

outside me

I remember a day when I was once again debating.

Marry him or not?

Why is that such a hard flipping question tumbling around within me like a marble ping-ponging against my spleen?

Sure he was French.
Hot.
And here.

But marriage?

I'd thought *maybe* once, but that had been long ago—a whirlwind affair that ended in tragedy.

So while not turned off,
I'd simply shut down that thought.

No weight to it being good nor bad.

I'd simply avoided the topic altogether, till now, as I didn't want to have to dive in and deal.

Simply not of importance to little old me.

The businesswoman focused on her growing business.

The writer forever living in her head.

The me afraid to open the box and truly feel.

Was there room for a full-time man?

Space for me to take on yet another role?

Wife? *Seriously?!*

All this poured out of me while seated on a conch house porch in the Florida Keys.

A new year, a lost me.

A moment of questioning everything.

Because internally, on some level, I knew being a wife conflicted with my value of free-bird me.

I'll never forget this moment with a then-girlfriend. She, a needle-thrower of sorts, loved to jab me and allow my *chi* (or is it *chai?*) to run free.

But on this day, it was my mouth jabbing away.

To the left, do I go?
Or to the right, do I stay?

The more I spoke, the more confused I became.

My words building webs, entrapping me, encasing me, until I felt the suffering folds of a cocoon engulfing me.

A vice-like grip my ribcage became, until even my breath struggled before deciding to come streaming out of me.

Hmm, how worked up was I that it took a beat for her words to settle upon me.

If it doesn't work out, just get a divorce.

And something in me clicked.

It was simply a matter of choice.

A choice in *that* moment.

Not in two, five, ten years down the road.

Not in the land of *what if* I was spinning faster than a spider spins an, early morning, *suddenly there web.*

While I'm not belittling the weight of *just get a divorce* and saying it's as easy as one-two-three decide,

I am sharing this—

Is it not a story to believe it, a divorce, anything has to be hard, painful, long, drawn-out, difficult, costly?

In that moment, I chose.

And now, nearly ten years later, I choose him each and every day.

Sometimes it takes a jab, a word, a friend, a coach,
another's voice . . .

One who resides outside
the ping-pong mess
of your head trash,
to shed light
on what's really within—

you.

to the left, to the right

Who do you listen to?

Which way do you go?

Talk about feeling conflicted when you just don't know.

This used to be my existence,
forever looking right then left.

Forever searching outside myself.

Asking others which way I should turn
and then being *resentful*,
feeling *annoyed, put out, upset, frustrated*
when it didn't work out.

Of course it's not going to work out 99.9 percent of
that time, because I was walking around *all but blind*.

So not aligned.

People from friends and family to downright strangers
will offer *their* perspective.

Girl, beware.

Their POV comes from the stories they have about
you. For they do. And the stories they have about
themselves.

Stories . . .

From their own programming
behind the curtain of them,
that is how *they* direct
your life scene.

What another person has to say will never serve you
100 percent or at all until you first tap into knowing
yourself . . .

which goes back to the sign above the Oracle's door
in the movie *The Matrix*—

Temet nosce.

Know thyself first *before* you ask for external
feedback.

And here's the delicious truth . . .

When you start to know yourself,
you will no longer feel called to ask another's opinion
about you,
about what you should or shouldn't do
or even *how* to do it.

You will no longer be seeking a voice other than
tuning into your own.

And if you do, when you do, it's with intention—
from a place of already quietly aligned.

And that's *divine*!

The question I am asked often is,

But how, Jill? How do I know what to do when I'm so used to asking everyone else?

Typically, I'd say *the how is none of your business,* however in this case, it is, because *the how is the way to you.*

ask me

Now when I want an answer, *I ask myself first.*

Hand to heart,
deep breath in,
slow breath out.

And when bells don't ring,
angels don't slip down from my tropical blue sky,
I don't get that knowing right away,
an answer, any answer I seek,
I give it no weight.

No thought.
No meaning of *not worthy.*

Instead, I let go, release, allow, wait.

Now willingly,
deliciously,
patiently.

If another day comes, I simply ask again,

Hand to heart, *deep breath in,*
slow breath out,

if I feel so called to.

The question in the forefront of my mind,
not dwelled upon . . .

Just asked once again and released.

Ask and dwell,
ponder and replay on repeat—
this was my old way of showing up.

Ask again and again,
Foot tap-tap-tapping an impatient beat.

That way will lead to a foul.
Game over before you even take the mound.

A surefire way to dim the lights on the stage of you
constantly missing your moment to take that cue.

Ask and *allow.*
Ask and *let be.*
Ask and *believe the answer has already come.*

Sink into knowing the answer will arrive *somehow,
someway.*

Not as expected, maybe . . .
So simply be willing to *play.*

I ask and I get quiet.
No doubt.

I ask.
I sleep on it.
Or walk it out.

I ask, then release.

Staying open, and present
to possibility.

unstoppable

When we accept everyone else's stories, even stories
that have nothing to do with us, it becomes hard to
hear our inner voice.

When someone says, *Go with your gut,* or
Trust your intuition,

that's tricky to follow
when you've spent years
drowning out your innate knowing.

Hearing instead the stories of others.

**How can you *know* yourself if you can't *hear*
yourself?**

This is everything.

This is what this book, this journey, is all about.

The writing, the *Purple Pen Practices* you may be
choosing to access and sink into,

all are about discovering *who you are.*

What it feels like to be the real you—unmasked.

To finally find your own unique voice, to be heard, seen.

No longer needing to so desperately be understood.

Seeing the stories,
peeling away those that chain you,
finding the ones that are true to you,
that serve *who you say you are* and *who you want to
be*—fully.

Becoming aware.

Which stories are serving you?
Which are not?

Letting them go.

Sitting in silence is about listening to that inner
voice . . .

Tapping into the feeling deep within.

Changing the way you
speak to yourself and about yourself . . .

Changing the stories you play
on repeat in your subconscious . . .

Writing out a new story of you.

A laying of the new foundation of you.

A foundation that is so solid you can begin today,
Saying No

For when you *Say No* to what no longer serves you that is *Saying Yes to yourself.*

And that right there is a delicious life-changing thang.

Asking yourself questions and waiting to hear the answer is learning to trust your intuition. It's learning to open your inner knowing and discovering that *all the answers you need are already inside you.*

To know what you want, you *must* first *know* yourself.

And most people do not.
Many are afraid to . . .

It is my desire that you lean into this, *fearlessly*.

That you are willing to be *bold* and *brave* and *bright*. An *unstoppable force.*

This is the journey.

The *Journey of You*—JOY.

Purple Pen
PRACTICE

ask yourself

Ask yourself a question that has been troubling you. Write down the question if it helps to see it in black and white.

Take a beat and don't seek out the answer right away.

When we pose a question and want an answer, we tend to become impatient.

We want a *one-click* option on the way to go, path to choose, right or wrong of that which we are overly eager to know.

When you have a question, imagine if you practiced the art of accessing your inner voice.

Oftentimes a whisper deep within.
A feeling.
A sensing.

Not necessarily heard but felt, seen, visualized.

Simply allow your inner knowing to reveal itself to you.

Not going outward to ask another but looking at the penned question you wrote down, the one tumbling in your mind, the one that has perhaps kept you up late at night.

- *Who am I?*

- *What do I even want?*

- *Why am I here?*

- *What is my purpose?*

- *What do I love to do?*

These are common questions so many sink into and all but drown in the spin of them.

Asking yourself looks like getting quiet, pressing pause on that desire to know *now, now, now*—

insert a foot stomp if you're anything like the old me.

Sit in silence until you hear your inner voice,
feel that spine tingle,
sense that inner knowing of *hell yes!*

If it doesn't happen right away, that's okay.

Instead, notice how quick you are to judge yourself for not getting it, not tapping in, not having a good enough intuition.

I say, stop it and check your hurry.

If you've been practicing the art of asking everyone under the sun what you should do, your *inner voice* might still be playing peekaboo with you.

Allow that dormant part of you to come out of hiding.

The more you demand an answer now, the more you turn down the dial.

Ask once and then let go. And know, with fierce freedom the answer will come when the time is best for you to receive it.

When you are open, willing, grounded . . .
No longer forcing, rushing, hurrying up an answer.

Walk away and come back to your question again later.

No need to dwell.
Simply release and allow your question to float away.

Not gone, simply being heard, received.

Allow the faith to know your answer to your ask is there for you, in you.

That is the work.

When that inner voice starts talking, and it will if you rock true and stop looking outside yourself to find you . . .

When that answer comes, start writing and see what unfolds as it might surprise you in the absolute simplicity.

You know more than you think and when you're ready, you'll tap into discovering the blessing that listening to you first and foremost is.

wealth. health. happiness.

Throughout my twenties and thirties, each night
before I fell asleep, I would whisper internally,
sometimes externally, "Wealth. Health. Happiness."

I don't know where I learned to do this,
how I chose those words.
It simply was a part of me.

A habit. A routine.

I just mumbled them each night as I fell asleep.
And smiled.
Because I believed them true.

What's funny is that wealth, as in money, isn't one of
my top values. But I was *supposed* to want it.

The American dream.

We all want to be rich.
We all want to be famous.
Do we?

Do you . . .
really?

What do you want?

Keep asking . . .

living by values

JOY is my highest value.

After JOY, the things I value are
freedom,
privacy,
anonymity,
downtime to be alone,

and *edification* of others.
Don't forget that because it's my backbone.

Raising up others.
Giving credit where credit is due.

And to do that as a lead singer of my own life,
on the stage of me,
no longer being the backup vocalist just to fit in—
to people-please

Well, that's what these pages are about.

This is my deep dive into realizing that I can have both
privacy and *show up as me.*

This is my swim in seeing that I can play in the currents
with others and not have to be dragged down, deep.

This is my time to bask in my slice of sunlight,
staying dry from the old stories that once soaked me,

made me so heavy I was unable to streak across my
tropical midnight sky.

When living by values, all becomes easy.

When living not to please another,
but being true to myself,
there is freedom

Because I claim it.

There is downtime to recharge
because I demand it,
take it,
and rock it.

There is JOY because it's my top value . . .

Makes the engine of me purr
even through the ebbs and flow,
the ups and downs,
the crazy-town times

of living this thing called life.

I choose to
make it,
see it,
receive it

as *delicious.*

contradiction

Many of my shares in these pages seem to contradict that need for privacy, and yet here's what I feel, see, and know.

I am here to serve.

I am here to make the world a better place by wielding my purple pen.

By coaching my amazing clients to find their own voices and shout their messages loud and proud.

To write the words, the story, another isn't able to craft on their own.

I am here,
the conduit for the words,
the message of the moment that flows through me.

I have always known the words are a gift.
Not mine to own.

Who am I to censor what comes through?

Who am I to scratch out this or that as too personal?

Who am I to hide behind a false front,
out of plain sight?

Who are you to do the same . . .?

If the words that flow through me,
the personal shares that grace these pages,
can help one, *then I have won.*

This is me getting out of my own way.
Are you ready to do the same?

This is me stepping outside the comfort zone of my past.

Modeling possibility.

I can still serve, share, and be aligned in JOY
and all the other values I hold dear . . .

Not fully bared
but *transparent,*
vulnerable,
real.

Sharing what I am called to share,
not out of a need to be seen, heard, loved, liked even
but because it feels *right.*

And maybe in those shares you will find hope.

A message to carry you into your own greatness—
to support you, guide you, help you
discover your own voice,
shed those stories you've owned for decades,
and purple pen delicious new ones that serve you.

spotlight

Much like my writing, most of my true JOYful nature was on lockdown, hidden away.

Pieces, parts would shine through—at times, but I was careful, alert, on edge.

Never fully sharing me, perhaps because it didn't feel safe, perhaps to people-please and tone it down, perhaps to not steal from another's spotlight.

Yet, one day, over a shared meal with my pseudo-family, in a private dining room of a restaurant in Boston, I sat unaware of my own shine.

Carly Simon's "You're So Vain" had been piped into the room, probably playing throughout the entire restaurant, and I got swept away in the tune as conversations rolled on around me.

I started to sing, which I was prone to do when content, happy, at ease and guess I hadn't paid attention to my *tone it down, Jill* story in that moment and allowed my natural JOY to shine through.

Great lyrics, great melody, I didn't notice the room had fallen silent as a half dozen conversations ceased and a good forty eyes swung my way.

Seated at the head of the table for some god-awful reason, I had been paying attention to pushing leftover food around my done plate, when I felt more than heard the sudden still-quietness of the room.

My eyes inching up, my voice still on high, I continued to sing as I met eye after eye after eye.

That feeling of caught, trapped, *oh-shit*
a leaded weight in my body but not my soul.

The song, the melody, that was a current part of me and something in me allowed it to play out . . .

"You're so vain. I bet you think this song is about you. Don't you? Don't you? Don't you?"

To belt out of me until I couldn't take the shocked, surprised stares.

Couldn't sit in the imagined heat of my own center stage spotlight a second longer.

So I did the only thing I could think to do. I flubbed the song in grand Barbara Streisand style.

I added a New Yorker twist, an accent, a deliciously awkward drawn-out note—and the tension in the room broke.

Suddenly, I was once again *Just Jill*.
The quiet girl lost in her own inner world.

Nineteen souls laughed, not at me, but with me.
For I started the *joke* with a half-hearted giggle.

And smiling eyes swung away from me one by one.

All except the hot stare of my pseudo-mom on my
right. Her single line vibrated in my head. "I didn't
know you could *sing*, Jill."

And then she, too, turned away. And it was okay.

I could draw in a deep breath, slowly relax my—
unbeknownst to me until then—
tense muscles and once again go within

My silent answer

"You don't know anything about me."

so wanted to take the mic and ricochet through the
space—but that just wasn't me.

Yet.

It wasn't until much, much later in life that I saw that
lack of knowing me wasn't *her* fault, anyone's fault, but
solely *my* responsibility.

Because my highest value at that time was to hide.

Purple Pen
PRACTICE

so high

What is your highest value?

Now that the question is posed,
the answers, the knowing, *will* start to unfold.

When you know it, lead from there and all else falls
into place. With grace.

From money
to family,
success
to abundance,
spirituality
to inner peace,
creativity,
to happiness,
to JOY . . .

There is a wide range of endless values upon which
to choose.

Simply try a few on.

Spend seven minutes just jotting down what's
important to you in your journal. This can be a list or a
way of being—*a characteristic*—like "artistic."

Take a break and then go back to what you wrote.

Making none "wrong" is the key to discovering you. This is where the work truly begins.

Pick one. Like mine is JOY.

What is the highest value or state you wish to operate from?

Imagine all the programs of you now running from this new, aligned place . . .

Doesn't that sound delicious?

ending fear

I'm sure it's safe to say that no one
in the history of man
ever put procrastination down
as a top value or skill . . .

Yet so many of us *live* as though it *is* . . .
constantly *dating* that way of being
until it's locked and loaded . . .

Do you really want to put a ring on it?

Stay married to this way of not showing up in your life?

I sure as hell didn't, so I did the only sane thing I could . . .

I stopped.

Stop procrastinating.

Procrastination is simply a way to avoid
doing that thing you fear.

We put off that which frightens us for another day. If
you want to change this, *start leaning into that fear*
and do the thing anyway.

Then ask yourself *what stories are there based in that fear?*

And see if they serve you or hold your fine ass back.

From there, you know what to do. Pick up that purple pen and craft a new version of you.

A new story that serves you could be

I walk into the fear.
I take one step at a time.
I do what I am called to do in this moment.

When you show up as one or all three of those stories, procrastination will be a thing of your past. And you will feel so incredibly free.

I know it. It has happened to me.

And I've watched it unfold for so many.

Jill, I want to write a book. Someday. I'm just too busy to do it.

If I had a dollar for every time I heard this, I'd be able to put a sizable down payment on a Writer's Cottage Island Retreat . . .

A place where wannabe or full-on artists could get out of their limiting beliefs and own their *I am a writer* dream.

This would be the land of *no excuses.*

Hmm, maybe I'll go ahead and do that! What an idea . . .

And that's how all we create begins.

With a thought, a dream,
typically, *for me,* not shared,
but now that the idea of a *Writer's Cottage Island
Retreat*, a place for the creative within to nestle in . . .

Now that the idea is out there,
verbalized on this paper or digital page . . .

Or playing in your ear.

Just wait . . . chances are *I will create it.*
Or someone will.

That's the power of an idea,
of your thoughts.

You are always *creating* . . .

So what specifically do you want to create in your life
today?

Let go of the excuses that pile up like Jenga pieces on
a slippery slope.

Because guess what?

You have time when you make time.

expecting . . .

When I let go of my expectations of All,
things shifted.

When I let go of my expectations of others . . .

of what I *should feel,*
of what I *should do,*
of how I *should have been treated* . . .

I start to feel the bottled-up emotions.

First as a crashing, breath-stealing wave.
An endless plunge,
a self-induced waterboarding of me.

Until one by one, I stopped getting drenched.
Instead I learned to name what it was I felt.

Name the feels.
Heal.

When you have no expectations around a thing,
there is *freedom* to *transform.*

You become more fluid,
able to see life in new ways.

There is no *shoulda, coulda, woulda.*

There is no *I failed because I missed a day at the gym.*
There is no *I cheated on my diet so there goes my
New Year's Resolution.*

Instead, what's possible when you choose to live from a place of

Does this support me?
This way of thinking, acting, feeling, speaking, creating?

And a simple *yes* or *no* is felt.

You now naturally lean into that which supports you fully, wholeheartedly because *you love yourself.*

You take your story one moment at a time.
No longer pulling on the push door of life.

Because, really, this moment is all you have.

For me, it helps to write it out. And perhaps it will for you too.

Write your story.

See the *expectations* in black and white. Or purple and white if you're like me and prefer your words in vibrant color.

See your expectations, and then
Let. Them. Go.

Now, tell your story with no expectations about *how it ends, pans out, evolves.*

What is, is.
The End.

How does *that* feel?

eleven

When I was in the fifth grade, I entered my *third* fifth-grade classroom, after moving across the country to live with my dad. It was unexpected, as was the entire topsy-turvy year, but that's another *story*.

This new-to-me teacher seemed fun even with glasses, a grin that turned his lip up on one side, almost hidden, but seen by me,
behind a trim, close-cut beard.

As the students craned their necks, leaning to and fro in their seats to get a look at the "new kid," I stared unflinchingly back.

Being the new kid can go one of two ways.

With you on the top,
Queen B.

Or you sucking wind by day's end
like you took a few swift kicks
to the gut.

This time, I was determined to end the day on top, as I'd had it both ways already this year.

So, this teacher, Mr. R., let's call him, took me by the hand and walked me to the front of the classroom after a quick side hug with my *so not* old man.

At first, I thought, *Crap, a desk in the front row.*

I preferred to observe. Hard to do from the head of the room.

But then we stopped by his desk and my heart dropped into my stomach, creating a ripple of nauseating waves that threatened to erupt out of me if I didn't push that shit down.

He turned to me and said, "Tell me your story."

I nearly passed out as I forgot yet again to breathe.

First minute, first day, and he was going to make me stand in front of the forty-plus eyeballs already trained on my back and share who I was while all sat *in judgement* of me.

Seconds from my vision dimming to black, I remember resisting the urge to push up my too-big-for my-face glasses and instead began to count backward from ninety-nine.

Sometimes that worked. I'd never once fainted yet knew there was a first time for everything.

He repeated the words, "Tell me your story."

But this time, he stood behind his desk chair and pulled it out with a scrape of legs against the old, worn linoleum floor. A palm up offering encouraged me to focus on the paper and pencil already set neatly . . .

for me?

Sucking in a deep breath, the tension drained out of my shoulders. My backpack in sudden jeopardy of sliding right off me.

The relief was a wave so glorious, I let the weight fall and smiled—an uncomfortable upturn of my normally straight-line, at that time, lips.

I quickly sat, before he could change his mind,
like adults tended to do,
and scooted closer to the desk.

When he nodded, I picked up the pencil,
gave him one more side-eyed glance,
and felt something within me slowly relax, unknotting deep inside as he quietly said,

"Write your story. Share or don't share. Totally up to you."

My lips in full, uncomfortable bloom, I hurriedly turned back to the blank page and felt such peace and JOY at being left the hell alone.

I got to work writing the waves of *thoughts, words, sentences, paragraphs* that were my life.

Fragments and tales and all the many shoved-down emotions. Feelings that had been bottling up within me for days, weeks, years . . . *a lifetime.*

That teacher, that man, gave me a gift that day.
An outlet.

A *write your story* moment more important than history, mathematics, or a spelling bee.

And I often dream of crossing paths with him

To thank him with a hug,
a handshake,
a kind *word* for taking the *time*,
for knowing just what I needed
in that moment
to *thrive*.

Survive.

Plus, it made me the *must-have* lunch companion when the time came, as everyone wanted to know why I was at the teacher's desk in the front of the class, not doing the assignments but busy working on something that *seemed* super important.

And it was. Important. Vital. Everything to me.

It was the first time I wrote *the story of me*.

My first memoir.

It wasn't about getting it right,
sharing what another wanted to hear,
writing regurgitated facts.

It was me being *perfectly imperfect* me.

review you

What if *perfect* doesn't exist? Does that set your life
suddenly on fire?

When I discovered that perfect doesn't exist,
the world hiccuped beneath my feet.
Literally.

I could have gone down the path of regret.
Bemoaned all the lost time
trying to get it *right*.

Focused on perfection.

Instead, I practiced what I preach.
I let go of what was and stepped home to a new
story—*of me.*

Kick perfect to the curb
as there's no such thing as perfection.

When you get this, the seas of *indecision* and
procrastination can part wide.

When you understand this,
and mix it together
with your own knowing
that *you are enough*
just as you are . . .

Even if it's fragile
and a new tale just being told . . .

Even if it doesn't always feel true-blue,
know that's normal.

Simply stay in it.

Focus on releasing what you do
instead of perfecting it again and again.

When you walk this way, your entire life *will* change.

This is a path to your most delicious life.

Dropping the need
to be *seen* as perfect,
to *produce* perfect,
to *believe* there even is a perfect.

Just be you.

And in these pages,
my belief, my dream, my desire
is you are starting to see who that is—*you*.

You are sinking into finding you.

Uncovering the you *long buried, masked, cloaked, hidden.*

When you do, you will release that thing you know is
within you.

Live that childhood dream,
write that book,
speak your peace—*loudly*.

Or in a soft, gentle tone.

One that will encourage ears to perk up,
bodies to lean in,
souls to gravitate toward *you*.

You will live *face forward*, no longer focused on the
rearview you.

This is what doing all things from a place of

100 percent is failure can offer you.

70 percent is the new perfect.

70 percent

When I was introduced to this concept, that 70
percent can be my new perfect, it changed all for me.

Suddenly life became a game of catch and release,
not catch and grip with an iron fist,
till I get it just right.

When we strive for what doesn't exist,
100 percent perfection,

which we are taught to do
in school, in life

we miss out on all
the enJOYment,
the fun,
the very point of living.

Forever sailing away, lights colorless and dim . . .

This is the snake eating itself,
the dog chasing its own tail . . .

The ship of you passing by
your own fine self,
your purpose.

Rudderless,
destination unknown,
as the focus is to spin yourself
again and again
into the most *perfect* of circles.

This is the snake eating itself,
the dog chasing its own tail . . .

An endless loop of seeking perfection.

And all you have to do today is hit pause and try on a
new way.

guidance system hits

When you are living your most delicious life,
you will receive hits,
an inner knowing,
of which path to take.

Which opportunity is best in this moment.

This is your natural GPS system.
Your *inner guidance* that will kick in
and share with you
exactly when to say *hell yes*.

And it will become easier and easier
to say *No, thanks*
to that which no longer serves you.

This comes when you *kick perfect to the curb of your life.*

From messages to coincidences . . .

You won't be able to make this shit up, as my UK
friend, a true goddess, likes to say.

Imagine the power of you
when you are attune, aligned, enough
in your mind
and so in sync with your most delicious life
you no longer allow in

negative thoughts,
fear,
procrastination,
the need to perfect.

And when they do show up,
sometimes you get to simply
whack-a-mole them away
with grace and a laugh,
saying, *No, not today!*

You know today is your day.

The very best day of you . . .
and that's where you focus all your attention,
your energy.

That's where you find you.

7: Living Your Story Out Loud

Living Your Story Out Loud

disclaimer.

Imagine if you *knew* . . .

You never need explain yourself.
Nor justify your story.

You tell your tale *if* and *when* ready.
Your way.

All you *are able to do*
with ease, grace, gratitude, and JOY
when you decide those ways of being matter—

is *live* it.

Your story.
Your journey.
Your life.

this moment

Begin today telling yourself new stories,
stories you want to live by.

And let go of the stories that
hold you back,
drag you down,
feel off . . .

No longer serve you.

BE YOU.

Who are you in this moment?

A new
awakening,
aware version
of fabulous you.

boxed in

People have opinions about. . .
pretty much everything.

People make judgements about, again,
pretty much everything.

It's what we delightful humans do.

We *label.*
We *categorize.*
We *box people in.*
Based on the lens in which we see life.

Remember how these pages, your very life, started?

We begin as a baby sponge,
absorbing all

And slowly,
day by day,
minute by minute,
hour by hour

the filters of different words we hear,
things we see, touch, and smell,
experiences we absorb,

all of those things individually
place filters over our fresh, innocent, unknowing—yet,
all knowing—eyes.

And these filters are like those programs that run in
the background of you—automatically.

Helping us label, categorize and box ourselves in when
we listen.

It's part of life.
It's what we do.
Learned behavior.

Don't make it right.
Don't make it wrong.
Allow it to just be what is.

Because now, now you can make a choice, reading
these lines, to become more aware.

Or not.

Aware of the preprogramming, the limitations shared
through another's view of life . . .

A parent's, teacher's, friend's, a foe's . . .

When we become aware,
and end our *judgy* suffering . . .

No longer feel a need to blame
others, our past,

or shame ourselves
for *not getting it sooner,*
for not having been smart enough
to see it in the first place . . .

Oh, that was so me!

Only then can we begin to shed
those filters, those labels, those categories—
stop running those automated programs—
and step free of the cage that has boxed us in.

Ready to do just that?

Turn the page, my friend.

bubble wrapped

Saying *yes* to you first,
that's the work.

Saying *yes* to

I know me,
I trust me,
I respect me,
I value me.

I love me.

Listening to that side of you more than you listen to
outside forces.

That's possible when you simply start
choosing what you *receive, allow in,*
and what you do not.

It doesn't mean others won't still happily share their
opinions, their thoughts about what you choose to do.

But it does impact the way in which you *react* or
choose not to when faced with another's injected
opinion of you, of your actions, of your life.

Imagine you get to erect a translucent bubble around
yourself.

A bubble that hears, feels, receives those words . . .

Another's thoughts,
energy,
emotional outbursts
before you do.

All first comes into contact with your outer bubble . . .

And when you feel up to it, ready, rooted in you . . .
you can accept parts or pieces to pass through to you
or reject all and return
the thought, words, idea, belief, emotion, energy
to the sender with love.

You get to press pause and actually see the thought,
the conversation, the judgement, the words pumping
and jumping against your delicious bubble.

This is your right.

This is your *two-foot space* around the entirety of
you, a see-through film that allows you to take *a beat,
a breath* and ask yourself if you want what's coming
your way.

If you even want to discuss it, let alone receive it.

A bubble that shimmers and glows with your inner
light and gives you room to choose.

Thank you, I receive that.

Or *thank you, but hell no, that one's for you to own.*

This you can whisper internally
and outwardly simply say,

I don't receive that.

Imagine if you simply spoke from your heart, what
often you say in your head but don't dare allow out as
you don't want to appear rude.

Girlfriend, someone will always find you rude or
lacking, fat or skinny, fabulous or perfect or imperfect.

The only question is

How do you find you?

When you find your voice and own your words of
No, thank you, I don't receive that . . .

The flower within you,
the seed planted before you were even born,
feels it's first rays of sweet sunlight.

Begin today, with your bubble around you,
to simply be you, however that may look and
ultimately be.

Feel the need for a bit more politeness in declining of
a comment?

As you begin to find your footing . . .

You can always say—

While I can appreciate your opinion,
I don't receive that.

I simply say, *Thank you, that's not for me to receive.*

But internally,
I'm a-saying it with more force
as a *Hell no.*

My mental shout-out is my way to remember loud and
clear—*I get to choose what I receive.*

Always.

This is your opportunity to begin to reject, at will,
that which is not about you,
that which you do not wish to hear,
that which does not serve you to even entertain.

You are allowed this.

You need never be *polite* or *ladylike,*
(whatever that even means!)
over being true to you again.

reflected reflection

Your bubble is about you granting yourself the ability to stand firm in who you are being, becoming.

Because guess what *Oh, Fab One* . . .

Most things others say to you have nothing to do with you.

Imagine that person sharing something with you about your body, your parenting, your dream not being realistic . . .

See them holding up an imaginary, ornate mirror that faces *their* reflection
not yours.

That mirror shows them speaking to themselves,
by speaking out loud to you.

Your bubble,
known only to you,
can be your layer of awareness
to start recognizing
the person talking to you is really speaking to their own reflection.

About their own weight,
their own parenting (now or in the past),
their own lost dream . . .

People, while well-meaning for the most part,
are about themselves first.

And that's not *good*, not *bad*,
that's instinct.

But for the empath,
the caregiver,
the people-pleaser,
who puts everyone
even strangers above herself . . .
himself . .

It's a lonely path of forever feeling

misunderstood,
undervalued,
not appreciated,
never validated . . .

Until you draw a line in the sand of you,
bubble wrap your sweet self,
and stand firmly planted in your newfound grounding.

When you do, you will no longer place so much
attention on what others think of you.

Because you will begin to understand that another's
opinions have nothing to do with you.

Another's opinions, thoughts, shares are *their stories*
to own.

Not yours to absorb, be impacted by
unless you so choose.

Start creating your bubble today
and wear it like a coat of arms.

Not to keep others out, at bay,
but to keep you firm in your knowing of you . . .

Until this new you is so solid
like a great oak whose foundation
is as widespread and rooted
as her shown, known branches.

Now that right there is delicious.

musical chairs

When your stories change, you change.
When you change, your circles will change.

Those in your current circles may move in and out.

It can feel hard, sad, lonely, a mess.
Or it can be seen as a natural tide of your life.

What would be possible if you didn't judge them or
yourself but instead simply stick to your path?

Know that those who no longer serve you,
this new higher vibe you,
the one who's got her own back . . .
well, they will fade away.

And it's okay.

It sucks *if you say it sucks.*
It hurts *if you say it hurts.*

Feel what you feel, but then move on—

Or you risk sinking into the quicksand
of old programs, tired worn-out stories
that no longer serve you.

You have a great idea for a business?

Someone may tell you all the things that could go wrong.

A fabulous idea for a book?

Someone just might try to rain on your parade, usually out of fear or jealousy.

You start shedding pounds as you, let go of story after story after story.

People often don't want you to change.
Most don't like change.

And if you change, *where will they be?*
Left out. Alone.

Unless they change too.

See the truth in another's insecurity when they go to hold you back, down,
keep you small.

That's about them,
not you.

It's not because they don't love you,
like you,
care about you . . .

but simply if you change they may just lose you.

Being ready to not become small again
just to please those who want you to remain the same,
that's part of this journey into creating your most
delicious life.

It might feel sucky.
But you being less you is worse.

And forever a story of your past.

not too anything

Living your life out loud means awakening to who you are. Shedding all the *well-meaning* and *mean* things you've heard said about you.

You're too sensitive, Jill.

Well-meaning, said out of love, perhaps.

Someone might believe *sensitive people are more easily hurt* and therefore these words are uttered with the utmost sincerity, simply wanting to protect.

Yet those words rolled around in me for nearly half a century. My choice, as I took them to mean something was wrong with me. *Broken. Not good enough.*

I gave those words power over me, which allowed me to doubt myself continuously.

Have you ever done the same with some such story said about you or to you?

I simply *am* sensitive. *Period.*
Not too. *Just enough.*

There are no mistakes in how we are created.

How you are made . . .

When you get this

and no longer see yourself as made
wrong, lacking, bad,
you will experience peace that, in and of itself,
is delicious.

Imagine moments where you no longer question
yourself, doubt yourself, wonder if you're doing the
right thing.

But instead, tap into the *freedom* to be fully, truly,
completely you.

Learning the skills to love this
too sensitive part of me
to no longer shame it, blame it,
make it bad, wrong,
a handicap . . .

That is what has allowed me to own my slice of
sunlight with JOY.

No expectations.
No attachments.

Just delicious sun on face, warmth on skin.
Ahhh! Heaven.

This is me.
See me.
Hear me.
Roar!

Thank you, Katy Perry, for giving women everywhere
the courage to do just that.
(Pop culture song reference for those not in the know.)

dopamine

If you want to get a hit of feel goods,
simply get up and *do that thing* you are called to do.

It's that little voice within that prompts you. *Listen.*
It may be an opportunity you've been waiting for. *Act.*

Work from the new story of *I love myself* that you've
been busy creating for yourself as you flipped through
the pages of this book.

Haven't started that daily work yet?

Saying *I love myself* on repeat till it's all you hear inside
your little old heady-head-head?

*What needs to happen before you make a choice to
sink in?*

*Before you do the thing that will change all in
your world?*

*What is it costing you to stay stuck in the stories of
not loving yourself?*

Another year—*gone.*
More struggling to make ends meet.

Another relationship.
More proof that you're a failure at love . . .

Come on now, that's nothing but a story you're *choosing* to keep alive.

Now's your time to *love you* enough to say, *No more!*

When you love you unconditionally you attract love to you. Like a bee to the sweet essence of you.

Another lost moment
to impact a life,
do what you love,
to finally fucking figure out what you actually want?

Positive reinforcement of your new story gives you a little shot of dopamine.

Oh yeah, the feel-good hormone.
Make mine a double.

That little voice *within*,
saying *get up and move your fine self,*

not the one that says
pull the covers up over your head.

That little voice is your new story-supporting drug of choice, if your new story is to be more healthy and fit.

And there will be a tug-of-war
between your old story of *lazy is me*
and your new reality.

This is your moment of utter, delicious truth.

The choice to walk down the new path
that leads to healthy
or stay stuck where you are,
saying you want something new
but not moving your feet to that fresh beat.

Not changing the *new, empowering* station you've
tuned into.

Not plugging back into the *lose faith* in you reruns.

The same channel you've perhaps played over and
over again.

If your story is—*My business is successful,*
you'll walk through the world
open to all the possibilities
for success and growth.

For abundance.

People will gravitate toward your energy.
Opportunities will come.

You will literally pull the best people toward you in
order to reach your goals, your dreams.

You will own your success as though it already is
(now).

Because it does already exist.

Like a box from Amazon,
once ordered

the pending delivery is an,
of course, no-brainer in your mind.

You *trust* completely in its arrival,
knowing, with faith,
that what lies in that box,
unseen by your eyes at this point,
does already in fact exist
and is on its merry way.

Catch that as it's gold,
all the moments you already know
you don't have to see something to believe it is.

Your words *create* the new story of you.
Your thoughts *support* that story.
Your voice *shares* that story again and again.

**The universe *reflects* you
and all you say.**

Mirroring your story,
sending you the energy
and opportunity
your way.

It may sound *woo-woo*, but it's simply Universal Law.

When you take what you receive
and move your feet
—*Hot damn!*—
you have a recipe
for massive deliciousness
in everyday life.

Because it's your actions,
based on who you are being
in your new story
that brings it all together,
creating your delicious reality.

your voice

Here's the deliciously good news.

You have a voice.
You were *gifted* a voice.
And now it's up to you to use it.

Even if you're
afraid,
nervous,
anxious.

It's okay!

You get to now *choose* how you wish to make your
voice sing.

In actual song or simply by *sharing* what is *true* to you
in this moment.

In any given conversation,
in business, in life,
on a stage, on a street corner,
in the pages of a book . . .

How divine.

**The path isn't as important as the next action
you take.**

The only thing that matters is you, in this moment,
with a choice to *Hush up now, you hear!*

Or the you ready to wave that crap off
and write a new, bold,
perhaps uncomfortable as fuck
story that *your voice does matter.*

State a new tale of *Hear me, loud and clear.*

You have a voice for a reason,
and it's time to own it, is it not?

the delicious reward

Did you know that when a hen lays an egg, she clucks? It's true!

She'll strut around,
ruffling her feathers,
flapping her wings,
clucking to the heavens,
celebrating the amazing thing she just did.

And the rest of the flock will follow suit, clucking and celebrating her accomplishment.

Imagine if you started to celebrate your accomplishments too. Daily.

Hens know what humans have forgotten—
there's enough sunshine for everyone. One hen's accomplishment does not diminish another's.

They never think it's *selfish* to toot their own horn.

In fact, *the louder the better.*

Yet when a human sings her praises, what does that make her?

 ➤ *Arrogant*

 ➤ *Selfish*

➤ *Stuck up*

➤ *Egotistical*

Hearing words, statements like,

➤ *Don't brag. It's not polite.*

➤ *Be a lady.*

➤ *Tone it down.*

➤ *No one likes a show-off.*

➤ *Ego much?!*

➤ *Well, aren't we full of ourselves?*

➤ *What a bitch!?*

Look at all the messed-up stories we have.

Stories that we pass down from *generation to generation.*

And these stories continue on
because we allow them to grow
and take root within us.

When you stop caring what another person thinks . . .

When you do what you do because it feels right to you in this moment . . .

You will be free.
You will feel JOY.

You will be living your most delicious life,
one you have created . . .
and that right there is divine.

And you will stop the cycle of passing
those stories down.

Down to your children,
grandchildren, a friend,
a stranger on the street.

This is the ripple of you knowing you, loving you, living
your most delicious life—*unapologetically*.

Not everyone will dance it out,
loud and proud,
in front of a large crowd
on the tabletop of their life.

And that's more than all right.

This is your life to live your way.

Simply stop looking to others before you choose how
to be.

Be you.

As these pages have shown you, this is your
opportunity.

celebrate

My way of celebrating
has always been to do so solo . . .

a giggle caught behind my own hand.

Hidden away to warm my heart on a day
when I perhaps wanted to give up.

Yet where is the ability to *receive* in that?
Lacking. . . perhaps.

And something I've personally been working on.

Even in writing these pages
as me,
in my voice . . .
with my story-shares.

Personal.
Perhaps profound.

I am stretching, growing, expanding, evolving.

I am allowing myself more.

Open*, willing to receive..*
From you, my delightful reader.

Not because I *need* to hear what you have to say.

Not because it *feeds* my soul to hear you celebrate these pages, these words.

Just as it will not tear me down to hear nothing, because to me crickets are one of the most beautiful of sounds.

Yet when we liken them to what we hear when no one shows, sings our praises up on loud

we diss mother nature,
we dismiss our own self-worth.

And that for me is a *no-go*.

I know, in my soul, this book, these pages *will* impact one. Thus, I have won.

Yet I am not attached to that outcome.

Before it's even released,
before I even finish writing these words.

In fact, my rooted intention as I write is that these words be like a rushing tide of awakening for hundreds, thousands, millions . . .

The impact felt for decades to come.

A sweeping across a land,
a soft breeze touching upturned faces.

Opening the hearts of all who are exposed,

a ripple more profound
than that of *The Butterfly Effect*.

My work is to write, to release, to allow the book room
to freely breathe.

And honor the reader, you, the space to enJOY or pass
on by.

The one who's ready will sink in and love these pages.

The one who's not may never see them or simply toss
them aside until the *right* time.

And either way is fine by me.

For I am not attached to an external, outside-of-me
outcome.

Instead, I focus on simply showing up daily, doing
what I love as the highest, best version of me.

Hear that and tap into your own *knowing*.

Your own passion, that thing you love—no second-
guessing.

When you do, you will know that your value, your
worth, does not come from the recognition of
your work.

Not even from the monetary gain, but from who you
are choosing to be.

My value, my worth is present
because I take the time daily to own it, celebrate it,
skinny-dip in it with delicious intention.

My celebration, my ruckus raised, my clucking
is in writing each and every day.

**What are you willing to celebrate right now,
loudly, in you?**

hugging JOY

It's not *right*. It's not *wrong*.
To shout out loud.

To hug your JOY close.
To keep it to yourself.

The truth is your JOY, your celebration of you, does
not take from someone else.

Your JOY is your own.

In fact, your JOY is an opportunity for others to
celebrate too.

Sharing who you are at your core, not with the
world, perhaps, but with those you choose. And first,
intimately with you.

When I am living in JOY, I attract others like a firefly.

My light is on
and people, deals, opportunities
come knocking.

Animals show up needing rescue,
which simply feeds my JOY.

When I am living in JOY,
I am abundant in all areas of my life because . . .

Abundance follows JOY.

And JOY is the Journey of You.

When we live our lives in JOY, others can feel that.

They may choose to accept that JOY,
bring it into themselves.

They may want some of that sunshine and ask you
how you got there.

Or they may run the other way . . . and it's okay.

Cluck for JOY! For you.

Share with them as much or as little as you wish of
your story. Of you.

Maybe let them borrow a copy of this book, or gift
them one, if it's helped you heal, grow, evolve, find
your own JOY.

spotlight moments

This is your moment to stand tall in the spotlight of you.

Whether you recognize it or not,
you now have a new story of you forming.

Maybe not fully created yet,
maybe only a framework,
a rough sketch,
but it's more *true* to you
than the mask of your past.

More *real* than the roles you've played.

Keep telling yourself your new story.

Remember, *positive and present tense is the magic.*

➤ *I love myself.*

➤ *I am good enough as I am.*

➤ *I am smart.*

➤ *I am creative.*

➤ *I am safe.*

➤ *I am a great mother.*

➤ *I am successful.*

When you can start to say these words,
any words that work for you,
and feel them deep within,
the utter knowing they are true will follow.

It may take time.

Have patience with you
and keep repeating positive
tales over and over again.

If you're anything like me, you had plenty of repetition telling yourself the negative stories. Whether you remember it or not, *it did take time for those to sink in* and become the truth you believed just yesterday.

Allow time for them to shed away . . .

A snake doesn't lose a layer of skin in a blink of an eye. He must first slither and slide and *feel* all the *ick* of *shedding* that which no longer fits him.

When you can own a saying like one my mentors shared with me and mean it bone-deep, know that your stories are a-shifting within.

Everything is fine because everything has been fine and will always be fine.

Simply stay in the pitter-patter of this new, delicious tune.

I love myself. I love myself. I love myself.

Stand in front of the mirror and repeat it over and over again as I did.

Spit toothpaste *everywhere*.
No thought to the mess.

It will take but a minute or two to clean up.

But the laughter that may just bubble up . . .

The JOY at being playful again
may just set you up for a delicious day
or relieve the tension of one all but done.

And that is the making of a most delicious life.

That mess is nothing to you.
Laugh at the messes you make.

Try it. I dare you.

How does it feel to laugh and smile and tell yourself
this new story centered in knowing what you want?

How does it feel to sink in to the truth that you are . . .

perfectly imperfect,
uniquely you,
worthy,
lovable,
loved,
enough . . .

your day

Take a beat and reflect on how you begin your day.

Do you *tap-tap-tap* away on a device first thing, reacting to *a like, an email, a text message?*

Do you start *wishing* you could pull the covers over your head?

Do you *greet* the day with a smile or a frown?

Do you *feel* delicious in your skin
or haggard, rundown?

Today is a new day to change the story of how your next day begins.

When you begin with a smile, it sets the tone.

Step back in time to the very first *Purple Pen Practice*, the creation of your Infinity Day goal.

That day is your gold-standard way of living. Magical. Not perfect. Simply perfect in its sheer imperfection because you choose to see it as such.

When you start with a stretch into pure gratitude for all that is, *it sets your vibe.*

When you rise up with love for you,

JOYful in what's to come,
knowing you got this,
whatever it is . . .

Guess what, boo? You do. You got you.

You are supported.

When you sink into this way of showing up for you each day,

Do share with me because *I want to celebrate you!*

Because in doing this work, *you are creating a new story* for how you choose to start your day.

And that right there is *everything*!

not the final curtain call

This is not the end between you and me
unless you choose it to be.

There is so much more in store for us
from what I can see.

And let me simply share that these essays are not the
only one's written.

There are enough for three if not four more books.

So if you have an interest in keeping our journey
together alive, do jump on the update train.

Make sure you're a part of my JOYful weekly
Wednesday Words.

So let me wrap this moment in time up,
complete with a purple ribbon and a virtual hug.

You. Are. Enough.

Thank you for taking a step down my *delicious word*
path and receiving that message in a big or small way.

I see you,
even through the pages between us because
everything is energy

and *your* energy matters.

8: More Delicious JOY

More Delicious JOY

Some would call this a references section.

I simply like to think of it as your own personal pot of gold found at the delicious non-end of this rainbow-bright Journey of You.

Because that's what you've accomplished thus far.

Whether you've read one essay or all 141 of them.

Whether you didn't notice a single *Purple Pen Practice* or dove into each and every one.

So let's start there.
In case you missed that delish memo!

All those Purple Pen Practices and so much more are yours to access in The Purple Pen Practice Handbook.

A free downloadable companion workbook complete with JOYful tips, exercises, and more of my words to support you on your journey through these pages and in your continued path of living your most delicious life.

Including a personal wrap-up essay of my writing of this book journey—found nowhere else.

Words you'll really want to sink your pearly whites into.

Because literally, we have only just begun.

And for me, that's fabulously divine.

If you feel the same, check out this one page of delights, where so much more is available to you after you download your handbook.

And check back often because I'm always adding more deliciousness.

social butterfly

If you'd like to spread your social wings and flutter them a bit, come connect with me online.

An Instagram fan, fabulous one?

@iamthejoyfulwriter

You can find me there sharing JOY, more words, baby goat pics and using #deliciouslifebook to dish all things this book.

And if you want a bit more interaction with me,
in a group or one-on-one setting,
you can find all those details on the special-access page.

Simply scan the QRcode on the last page or type in the website URL.

There are multiple ways that my words can support you in creating your most delicious life.

And they can all be found on The JOYful Writer's website.

And if you're looking to perhaps work one-on-one with me, you can find all those details in the "More Delicious JOY" section. But first, one more shout-out is needed here.

Great Full

Earlier in these pages, I spoke to values and living from them.

JOY is my default setting, JOY is my highest value.

When I am aligned in JOY,
all works in my life with ease.

When I'm not, I slip into frustration. That is my tell. We all have one. But that conversation is for another day.

These words are about *another* value I hold dear.

Living in *gratitude* and giving *credit where credit is due* by acknowledging another's impact on me, those are ways of being I live by—oh-so high up on the values of me.

There are two people who have impacted my life, given me the tools, the mirror to see my own courage, fortitude, self, so that I might choose to step into my slice of sunlight.

I've mentioned them throughout the pages of this book as *my mentor* and *my coach*. Now it's time to shine a spotlight on each of them.

mentor

First, my mentor, through whom I learned the absolute importance of aligning with my values. His name is Jim Fortin, and he runs a program called *The Transformational Coaching Program*.

In January 2019, I enrolled in this program and by mid-February, I saw clearly that I was buried under the stories of me, of others, of the world.

This man put me in *time-out* just a few weeks in, because I was forever asking *why?*

Forever spinning in my head, overthinking every minute detail, struggling to analyze my way to the transformation of me.

Not even realizing how much
I hated me,
thought *I wasn't enough*,
felt life was *out to get me*,
that I was *being punished*
for something I had done,
simply for who I be . . .

This man, with a wealth of knowledge and deep-seated love to impact as many lives as he can, has definitely impacted me.

So much so that I knew I'd be a coach in his online, twice-a-year program, and *so I was*. The power of intention, he shed light on that for me too.

This man helped glue together so many puzzle pieces of "self-help" that I understood but didn't know or couldn't fit together myself.

It was in Jim's program that *I first wrote as me, received feedback as me, stopped hiding me.*

I am forever grateful to Jim as he changed the course of my life . . . and introduced me to my coach. More on her in one moment.

If you want to tap into what my mentor offers and hear for yourself what he has to say, please tune in to his podcast, *The Jim Fortin Podcast*. It's phenomenal.

Press play on episode one, and perhaps, like mine, your life will never again be the same, *mundane*.

coach

Now, the reason I give that man, Jim, my mentor, so much credit for the impact he's had on my life is because he introduced me to an amazing woman, who in January 2019 was and still is a coach in his *Transformational Coaching Program*.

She is also a master high performance coach in her own right, with an amazing high-touch, in-demand practice working with overachievers and deep-feelers.

Because she walks the walk, does the work, and checks some of the same value boxes as I do—one of them being personal *integrity* and *intimacy*—I stepped up to *the plate of discomfort* and hired her in August 2020.

Her name is Lisa Carpenter, and her coaching business is called Full Frontal Living™—also the name of her podcast, which I'd encourage you to listen to. And two years later, at time of publication, she is still my coach.

She's simply *that* good at shining a spotlight on my dark nooks and blind-spot crannies.

Lisa is a woman who *feels deeply, loves profoundly, and impacts greatly*. She taught me that my way of being—*of feeling my way through life, being an empath*—was not wrong unless I labeled it as such.

She helped me see that *feelings expressed are powerful, empowering, beneficial.*

She encouraged me to express myself,
learn to name my feelings,
and step into my slice of sunlight—as me.

Not as a people-pleasing chameleon.
Not stuffing my feelings down.

No longer needing to hide in plain sight.

So if equal credit is due for my name being on the front page of this book, it goes to her, for without her guidance at this time in my life, I'd still be very happily hiding little old me.

This work, this book, these pages, all these words are dedicated to Lisa.

While the energy of a group program, an aligned community, that was life-changing for me, it was the one-on-one work that really allowed me to *transform me.*

The power of a personal coach, a one-on-one approach, is something that cannot be ignored. When the time is right for this in your life, you will know.

For me to go from hiding in plain sight to full-frontal living—well, enough said, for now . . .

seasons

Life has seasons; we know this, as even on a tropical island we experience them. Perhaps not as much as we would closer to the North or South poles, but *seasons exist, and they teach us much* if we are willing to tap in.

I am in a new season of my life
as I am no longer hiding my light,
giggling quietly behind my hand,
living in the shadows of this life
but instead, stepping out—
as me.

And it started this year with choosing my own name
as my word of 2021 as you have read in the pages of
this book.

And it will continue in early 2022
with a delicious purple celebratory bow
when these words are published . . .
available to any,
to all,
to read,
sink into,
enJOY,
to own.

Because once I hand these pages off, my part is done. My season with these words is over.

Yet, these words, these pages, these essays, in the order read, polished so brightly, would not have been possible without Autumn.

Like a graceful gazelle, Autumn (Star) Sullivan, raced into my *word*-life as my new editor. [*Thank you, Michael.*]

Yet sleek as a fox, the season of she quickly morphed into a delicious sister-in-lit-crime, cohort, friend.

I am blessed to be surrounded by such loving support in this new season of my writer's journey with this amazing woman, who has taken my words and made them her own lullaby baby.

Not once hushing, shushing but encouraging them to sing, to bling.

Thank you, Autumn. I raise my morning mug of green tea to you in blessed gratitude.

And my glass of wine to you *this* night . . .
As these words sail on,
out of my sight, our sight,
to their awaited reader-destiny.

So many more delicious *word*-journeys with you,
my word-wielding, newfound friend.

oh-so real deal

There are a few more shout-outs that must be given by me before I call this a wrap.

And they include one lady who was so honest-to-God-real that I paid attention. She actually made me sit up and think, *What if I too could be that comfortable, confident, good in my skin?*

Kim Constable is an Irish lass who knows herself so damn well, is so bloody confident, and doesn't give two shits if you love her or hate her.

And that way of being—

no attachment to how another sees you, reacts to you, likes you or doesn't.

That right there is everything.
To be so good with yourself,

so self-aware that you auto-correct based on your own needs, not another's—
powerful.

Plus, this woman, also known as *The Sculpted Vegan* and *The Million Dollar Mentor*, is a dynamic storyteller who loves people, loves to impact, and is 100 percent transparent and real.

From one storyteller to another, *thank you.*

Thank you for posing just the *right* questions at just the *right* time.

shout-outs

For the father who has always been the rock in my turbulent sea. I loved you fearlessly, deeply, completely as a child. As a woman, I love the intelligent, sensitive man I see you to be.

For the more-than-friend you have always been, you know who you are. From brushing my hair as a painful girl to listening to me bemoan my fate, you have always supported and loved me, even when I wasn't easy.

While first in my life, *after Moo Baah the Goat*, of course, my Frenchman is the last I need to shout-out specifically and thank.

Even when I can forget his birthday while lost in my *word*-world, he stands by me.

He never keeps score—even when I once did.

Instead, he gives 100 percent and expects nothing in return. His choice. To simply love all of me even when I looked at him and honestly thought—*Why me?*

Through my ups, my downs, my flaws, my JOY, he supports me, loves me—for me.

The Fabulous Frenchman has been my greatest mirror and I am where I am today, living my childhood dream in a cottage overlooking the sea where I sit all day and write, in part, because of he.

I love you, Baby Babe.

There are others to thank and cover a few dozen pages in ink, but really, there is no need.

You know who you are and what you have meant to me.

What you mean to me still.

From family to friends to clients to students, you better me.

Thank you.

Jazz Hands

When we take things too seriously, we tend to lose the JOY that is our birthright.

The last thing I'd have you do is take my words, me, über seriously. This is your moment to take in what works for you, what resonates deeply, and toss the rest.

Perhaps to return to it again. A newer version of you, where something in the pages might now ring true . . . or not.

As for me, I'm a writer, a life-long learner, a student simply feeling my way through life and purple-penning what inspires me.

I'm Just Jill, with Jazz Hands, a few dance moves, and the ability to drop a beat at any moment.

And I'm living my most delicious life . . . what I want for you, if you want it too.

My childhood dream
of a little cottage on a hill surrounded by secret gardens overlooking the sea
where I sit all day and write.

Jill

just jill

So this is awkward, writing as third-person me, but let's play, shall we?

Jill R. Stevens has been a ghostwriter for almost three decades, devoted to shining a spotlight on the stories, messages, words of another, while quietly purple-penning her own tales under pseudonyms.

She's been consulting for twenty years with authors, both new and seasoned, to help them find their voice and shine. Jill also privately coaches a handful of clients at a time.

Mostly though, Jill writes. *Endlessly. Prolifically.*

Jill's new editor, Autumn, is currently shaking her head in part disbelief, part delight. See, this one book is *the first in five* that will be released over the coming year. Not planned, simply the product that came from being the conduit for one. Yep, more than 100,000-plus words—*unable to be contained.*

She does actually live in the middle of the sea, on an undisclosed tropical island, with heavenly breezes and a one-eighty view most only dream about.

When Jill is not writing, she is working on her island cottage, still under renovations three-plus years in, and rescuing baby goats. She's up to nine bottle babies at the time of this publication and is considering starting a foundation or fundraiser to support her efforts.

Animals (and children) gravitate to Jill and are her inspiration for writing all the words.

Beware, if you turn on the radio, it may just be some delicious words of hers you head-bop to.

Ain't no genre that can hold this girl's SuperPower down.

For more Jill, JOY, and *Jazz Hands* in your life, jump on her weekly email newsletter*

---

* https://www.thejoyfulwriter.com/wednesday-words

417

my ask of you—a review

Simply put, please write a delicious review.

Leaving a five-star review on Amazon
and sharing the impact this book has had on you
could change another's life . . .

And may result in even more abundant, delicious JOY
for you.

Because *everything is energy after all.*

When you put out good,
good must return back to you—
10, 100, 1000 fold.

So if this book
moved you,
inspired you,
made you mad—
for just a tad moment in time

If my words
brought out a smile,
a newfound glow

Helped you in some big or small way, share that today.

With a friend, coworker, family member, stranger on
the street.

You never know who or how your action will impact.

But it will. It does. Because *you* matter.

You can also email me directly at
delicious@jillrstevens.com
and share with me your JOYful note.

When you give a dash of JOY, you create a ripple that
has no choice but to splash back upon you.

Coming Soon . . .

A new title by
JILL R. STEVENS

The Journey of You

A new title by
JILL R. STEVENS

Wife Waters

Made in the USA
Coppell, TX
15 March 2022

75043001R00249